Antisystemic Movements

Antisystemic Movements

GIOVANNI ARRIGHI,
TERENCE K. HOPKINS &
IMMANUEL WALLERSTEIN

VERSO

London · New York

First published by Verso 1989
© Giovanni Arrighi, Terrence K. Hopkins and Immanuel Wallerstein 1989, 2011

3 5 7 9 10 8 6 4

Verso
UK: 6 Meard Street, London W1F 0EG
US: 20 Jay Street, Suite 1010, Brooklyn, NY 11201
www.versobooks.com

Verso is the imprint of New Left Books

ISBN-13: 978-1-84467-786-3

British Library Cataloguing in Publication Data
A catalogue record for this book is available from the British Library

Library of Congress Cataloging-in-Publication Data
A catalog record for this book is available from the Library of Congress

Printed in the US

To our colleagues, in memoriam:

Aquino de Bragança
Ruth First
Georges Haupt
Walter Rodney

Contents

Acknowledgements

This set of essays is the fruit of a collaboration of many years and primarily of our joint participation in the annual International Colloquia on the World-Economy sponsored by the Fernand Braudel Center for the Study of Economies, Historical Systems, and Civilizations; the Maison des Sciences de L'Homme; and the Starnberger Institut zur Erforschung Globalen Strukturen, Entwicklungen, und Krisen. The first four essays were presented respectively at the IVth Colloquium, New Delhi, January 4–6 1982; the VIth Colloquium, Paris, June 4–5 1984; the VIIth Colloquium, Dakar, May 20–22 1985; and the VIIIth Colloquium, Modena, June 14–16, 1986. The last paper was given at the XIIth Political Economy of the World-System Conference, held at Emory University, Atlanta, March 24–26 1988.

All five essays have been previously published and are reprinted with permission: Essay 1 – *Review*, VI 3, Winter 1983; Essay 2 – *Social Research*, LIII 1, Spring 1986; Essay 3 – *Review*, X 3, Winter 1987; Essay 4 – *Review*, XII 2, Spring 1989; Essay 5 – in T. Boswell, ed., *Revolution in the World-System*, Greenwood Press, Westport, CT, 1989.

Introduction

The concept of antisystemic movements is one which presumes an analytic perspective about a system. The system referred to here is the world-system of historical capitalism which, we argue, has given rise to a set of antisystemic movements. It is the contours of this process that we are proposing to outline here. We are in search of the system-wide structural processes that have produced certain kinds of movements and which have simultaneously formed the constraints within which such movements have operated.

The movements have had their own mode of self-description. This self-description emerged largely out of categories that were formulated or crystallized in the nineteenth-century capitalist world-economy. Class and status-group were the two key concepts that justified these movements, explained their origins and their objectives, and indeed indicated the boundaries of their organizational networks.

The contemporary dilemmas of these movements are part and parcel of the same problem as the dilemmas of the concepts of class and status-group. That is why we felt that we could not analyze the movements, either historically or prospectively, without first rethinking these two concepts from a world-systems perspective.

We shall not repeat in this introduction the arguments that are to be found in the articles. We would merely like to suggest that if the structural processes that gave birth to these movements have been world-scale from the beginning, the organizational responses hitherto have been predominantly at the level of the various states. It is because we believe that new organizational responses will begin to surface that will be more world-scale that we think it urgent, not only for theory but for praxis, to reexamine the patterns and the degree of success of the world-system's antisystemic movements heretofore.

1

Rethinking the Concepts of Class and Status-Group in a World-Systems Perspective

In his well-known but often neglected conclusion to Book I of *The Wealth of Nations*, Adam Smith defined the interests of "the three great, original and constituent orders of every civilized society," that is, those who live by rent, those who live by wages, and those who live by profit (1961: I, 276). His argument was that the interests of the first two orders coincide with the general interest of society because, according to his analysis, the real value of both rents and wages rises with the prosperity and falls with the economic decline of society. The interests of profit earners, on the other hand, are different from, and even opposite to, such general social interest, because to widen the market and to narrow the competition are always in the interest of merchants and manufacturers. And, while to "widen the market may frequently be agreeable enough to the interest of the public; . . . to narrow the competition must always be against it, and can serve only the dealers, by raising their profits above what they naturally would be, to levy, for their own benefit, an absurd tax upon the rest of their fellow-citizens" (1961: I, 278).

Profit-earners not only have an interest contrary to the

general one. They also have a better knowledge of their interest and a greater power and determination in pursuing it than those who live by either rent or wages. The indolence of landowners, "which is the natural effect of the ease and security of their situation, renders them too often, not only ignorant, but incapable of that application of mind which is necessary in order to foresee and understand the consequences of any public regulation" (1961: I, 276–7). As for the wage-earner, "he is incapable either of comprehending the general social interest, or of understanding its connection with his own" (1961: I, 277). Moreover, in the public deliberations, "his voice is little heard and less regarded, except upon some particular occasions, when his clamour is animated, set on, and supported by his employers, not for his, but their own particular purposes" (1961: I, 277). Profit-earners, on the other hand, particularly those who employ the largest amount of capital, draw to themselves by their wealth the greatest share of the public consideration. Moreover, since during their whole lives they are engaged in plans and projects, they have a more acute understanding of their particular interest than the other orders of society.

The Wealth of Nations being a work of legislation, the purpose of this "class analysis" was to warn the sovereign against the dangers involved in following the advice and yielding to the pressures of merchants and master manufacturers. As the head of the national household, he should instead strengthen the rule of the market over civil society, thereby achieving the double objective of a more efficient public administration and a greater well-being of the nation.

It is not our purpose here to assess the soundness of the advice given by Smith to the national householder or of the substantive analysis on which it was based. Rather, we want to point out those aspects of his analysis that can be considered as paradigmatic of political economy and that we can find duplicated in contemporary class analyses.

First, the tripartite social order of which he spoke was a predicate of a particular kind of society; that defined by the territorial reach of a definite sovereign or state. These were the states of Europe as they had been and were being formed within mutually exclusive domains operating within an interstate system.

Second, his social orders (or classes) were defined on the basis of property relations. The ownership of land, of capital, and of labor-power define his three great orders of society. Among the proprietors of capital, what some today would call a "fraction" of capital (merchants and master manufacturers) is singled out for special treatment in view of its political–economic power, of its greater self-awareness of its own interests, and of the opposition of its interests to the general social well-being.

Third, the interests of each of the social orders/classes were identified with its market situation; that is, both their competitive opportunities in relation to each other as classes (and of individuals within each class to each other), and the costs and benefits to each of them of monopoly power within markets, understood as restriction of entry. In *The Wealth of Nations*, Smith limited the subjective ground of collective action by a class to these market interests. Monopoly power in the product as well as in factor markets was traced back to the creation of tolerance of restrictions to entry on the part of the sovereign/state.

Fourth, market relations were defined within or between national economic spaces. Class conflicts and alignments were thus limited to struggles within each state for influence/control over its policies. The unit of analysis, in other words, was the nation-state, which determined both the context and the object of class contradictions.

Fifth, a "relative autonomy" of state actions in relation to class interests and powers was presupposed. The enactment of laws and regulations by the state was continuously traced to the powers and influence of particular classes or "fractions" thereof. But the sovereign was assumed to be in a position to distance himself from any particular interest to promote some form of general interest, reflecting and/or generating a consensus for this general interest.

If we contrast this analytical framework with that associated with Karl Marx's *critique* of political economy (that is, of Smith and other classical economists), we notice two consequential shifts of focus: a shift away from state-defined economic spaces to world-economic space on the one hand, and a shift away from the marketplace to the workplace on the other.

The first shift implied that the market was no longer seen as enclosed within (or "embedded" in) each nation-state as an independent economic space, and that the world-economy was no longer conceived of as an interstate economy linking discrete national economic spaces. Rather, nation-states were seen as jurisdictional claims in a unitary world market. By effecting the socialization of labor on a world scale, the world market determined the most general context of the class contradictions and therefore of the class struggles of capitalist society, which Marx defined by its constitutive orders, the bourgeoisie and the proletariat:

> The modern history of capital dates from the creation in the sixteenth century of a world-embracing commerce and world-embracing market (1959: 146).
>
> This market has given an immense development to commerce, to navigation, to communication by land. This development has, in its turn, reacted on the extension of industry; and in proportion as industry, commerce, navigation, railways extended, in the same proportion the bourgeoisie developed, increased its capital, and pushed into the background every class handed down from the Middle Ages (1967: 81).

This was not a mere matter of trade relations between sovereign states. Rather, the developing bourgeoisie compels all nations, on pain of extinction, to adopt the bourgeois modes of production; it compels them to introduce what it calls civilization into their midst, i.e., to become bourgeoisie themselves. In one word, it creates a world after its own image (1967: 84).

The world so created was characterized by a highly stratified structure of domination and had more than market interests as subjective grounds for collective action:

> Just as it has made the country dependent on the towns, so it has made barbarian and semi-barbarian countries dependent on the civilized ones, nations of peasants on nations of bourgeois, the East on the West (1967: 84).

The second shift implied that the antagonism between the two great classes into which, according to Marx, bourgeois society as a whole tends to split, the bourgeoisie and the proletariat, was no longer traced to relations in the product or factor markets but to relations in production. In order to define the interests of the nation and of its component classes, Smith took leave of the pin factory whose scenario opens *The Wealth of Nations* to follow the interplay of supply and demand in the marketplace, and of class interests in the national political arena. Marx in his critique of political economy took us in the opposite direction. We take leave not of the shopfloor but of the noisy sphere of the marketplace (and, we may add, of the political arena) "where everything takes place on the surface and in view of all men," and follow the owner of the means of production and the possessor of labor power "into the hidden abode of production, on whose threshold there stares us in the face 'No admittance except on business'" (1959: 176). In this hidden abode of production, Marx discovered two quite contradictory tendencies that implied two quite different scenarios of class struggle and social transformation.

The first was the one generally emphasized in Marxist

literature after Marx: even if we assume that in the marketplace the relationship between the owners of the means of production and the owners of labor-power appears as a relationship between equals, in the sense that the commodities they bring to the market tend to exchange at their full cost of production/reproduction (which, of course, is not always or even normally the case), the relationship would still be a fundamentally unequal one. This is so because of the longer-run effects of capitalist production on the relative value and the relative bargaining power of capital and labor. Capitalist production, that is, is seen as a process that tends to reduce the value of labor-power (its real costs of reproduction) and simultaneously to undermine the bargaining power of its possessors, so that the advantages of the reduction of labor's costs of reproduction tend to accrue entirely to capital.

This tendency obviously poses problems of realization of the growing mass of surplus labor that capital appropriates in production. These problems periodically manifest themselves in crises of overproduction that are overcome on the one hand

> by enforced destruction of a mass of productive forces; on the other, by conquest of new markets, and by the more thorough exploitation of the old ones. That is to say, by paving the way for more destructive crises, and by diminishing the means whereby crises are prevented (1967: 86).

It would seem from the above that the unequal relation between labor and capital, continuously reproduced and enhanced in the workplace, leads capital either to self-destruction in the marketplace or to a greater development of the world-economy, both extensively (incorporations) and intensively. Given a finite globe, the more thorough this development, the greater the self-destructiveness of capital.

In this scenario labor plays no role in precipitating capitalist crises except in a negative sense; it is its growing subordination in the workplace, and consequent weakening of bargaining power in the marketplace, that are ultimately responsible for the outbreak of the "epidemic of over-production," as Marx called it. Labor, or its social personification, the proletariat, plays an active role only in transforming the self-destructiveness of capital into political revolution. The increasing precariousness of working and living conditions induces proletarians to form combinations against the bourgeoisie.

> Now and then the workers are victorious, but only for a time. The real fruit of their battles lies, not in the immediate result, but in the ever-expanding union of the workers . . . .
>
> This organization of the proletarians into a class, and consequently into a political party, is continuously being upset again by the competition between the workers themselves. But it ever rises up again, stronger, firmer, mightier . . . .
>
> Altogether collisions between the classes of the old society further, in many ways, the course of development of the proletariat. The bourgeoisie finds itself involved in a constant battle. At first with the aristocracy; later on, with those portions of the bourgeoisie itself, whose interests have become antagonistic to the progress of industry; at all times, with the bourgeoisie of foreign countries. In all these battles it sees itself compelled to appeal to the proletariat, to ask for its help, and thus, to drag it into the political arena (1967: 90).

Alongside this scenario, however, as we indicated, Marx suggested another one, quite distinct in its unfolding. Both in the *Manifesto* and in *Capital* we are told that, along with the growing mass of misery, oppression, and degradation, the strength of the working class grows too, not so much as a result of political organization aimed at counteracting its structural weakness, but rather as a result of the very process of capitalist production.

> Along with the constantly diminishing number of the magnates of capital . . . grows the mass of misery, oppression,

slavery, degradation, exploitation, but with this too grows the revolt of the working-class, a class always increasing in numbers, and disciplined, united, organized by the very mechanism of the process of capitalist production itself (1959: 763).

The essential condition for the existence, and for the sway of the bourgeois class, is the formation and augmentation of capital; the condition for capital is wage labor. Wage labor rests exclusively on competition between the laborers. The advance of industry, whose involuntary promoter is the bourgeoisie, replaces the isolation of the laborers, due to competition, by their revolutionary combination, due to association. The development of Modern Industry, therefore, cuts from under its feet the very foundation on which the bourgeoisie produces and appropriates products (1967: 93–4).

Here, therefore, the strengthening of labor in the workplace is the cause of the crisis of capital.

As we know, Marx never managed to reconcile these two contradictory tendencies that he discovered in the abode of production, let alone to work out fully and systematically all their implications for the analysis of class contradictions in capitalist society. Instead, Marx, in some of his historical writings, and many followers in their theoretical writings, gave up the critique of political economy and reverted to the Smithian paradigm of class analysis, reviving rather than carrying out the critique of political economy.

In the case of Marx, this retreat is most evident in his writings on the class struggle in France, in which class interests were defined in terms of a national political–economic space, and what goes on in the abode of production simply does not come into the picture at all. Obviously, Marx himself thought that the shift of focus he was advancing to analyze the overall, long-term tendencies of capitalist society had a limited relevance for the concrete analysis of a concrete instance of class struggle at a relatively low stage of development of such tendencies.

Moreover, even at the theoretical level, the shift of focus away from the noisy sphere of political economy did not imply any belittlement of the nation-state as the main locus of political power, that is, of the monopoly of the legitimate use of violence over a given territory. This power embodied in nation-states, whatever its origins, could obviously be used, and has indeed generally been used, simultaneously in two directions: as an aggressive/defensive instrument of intra-capitalist competition in the world-economy, and as an aggressive/defensive instrument of class struggle in national locales. True, the growing density and connectedness of world-economic networks on the one hand, and the displacement of class contradictions from the marketplace to the workplace on the other, would ultimately make nation-states "obsolete" from both points of view. In outlining this tendency, however, Marx was only defining the situation that the capitalist world-economy would asymptotically approach in the very long run. The farther the class struggle was from the projected asymptote, the more it would take on a political/national character. Even the proletariat, the class which in his view had neither country nor nationality, had first of all to wage a national struggle:

> Since the proletariat must first of all acquire political supremacy, must rise to be the leading class of the nation, must constitute itself *the* nation, it is, so far, itself national, though not in the bourgeois sense of the word (1967: 102).

Marx's empirical retreat into political economy did not, however, entail a corresponding retreat at the theoretical level. It simply implied a recognition of the distance separating the historical circumstances of nineteenth-century Europe from the asymptotic circumstances projected in the *Manifesto* and in *Capital.*

Far more than this was implicit in the retreat into/revival

of political economy by Marxists after Marx, however. The most striking characteristic of the *theories* of finance and monopoly capital, of imperialism and of state capitalism, that begin to develop at the turn of the century and are later synthesized in canonical form by Lenin, is that they take us back to the noisy sphere of political economic relations. Their main concerns are the forms of capitalist competition, and the class contradictions identified are those defined in terms of market interests and state power. However much such formulations may or may not be justified in terms of the political strategies of the time, we are concerned here with their elevation by epigones into theoretical advances rather than pragmatic retreats from Marx's critique of Smithian political economy.

This theoretical retreat into political economy had some justification in the tendencies that came to characterize the capitalist world-economy around the turn of the century. The growing unity of the world market presupposed by Marx's paradigmatic shift began to be undermined by the re-emergence of state protectionist/mercantilist policies. These policies increasingly transferred world capitalist competition from the realm of relations among enterprises to the realm of relations among states. As a consequence, war and national/imperial autarky came to the fore and in pragmatic terms shaped the scenario of the world-economy. Connected with this tendency, the high concentration and centralization of capital, characteristic of most of the new leading/core sectors of economic activity, led to a resurgence of practices, often backed by state power, that restricted competition within the national/imperial segments into which the world-economy was splitting. States thus returned to the forefront of world-economic life, and monopoly in and through the sovereign became once again the central issue around which conflicts and alignments among classes and fractions thereof revolved. This situation, which has broadly characterized the first half of the twentieth century, undoubtedly warranted a revival of political economy as the most relevant theoretical framework for the short- or medium-term analysis of class contradictions and conflicts.

We should not be surprised, therefore, to find that the conception of class conflicts and alliances advanced by Lenin fits better theoretically into the Smithian than the Marxian paradigm: the monopoly power of a "fraction" of capital (finance capital and large-scale industry, as opposed to Smith's merchants and master manufacturers employing large capitals) is singled out as the main determinant of waste and exploitation as well as of inter-imperialist rivalries and war (the enmity among nations, in Smithian parlance). It follows that all "popular classes," including the non-monopolistic fractions of capital, can be mobilized by the party of the proletariat (the "new prince," as Gramsci would have said) to wrest political power from the monopolistic fractions of capital — a prescription analogous to Smith's suggestion that the enlightened sovereign could count on the support of all other orders of society in pursuing the general interest against the particular interest of large merchants and manufacturers.

This, however, is not all that was involved in the theoretical retreat of Marxists back into political economy. Monopoly capitalism and imperialism were not treated for what they ultimately turned out to be — a cyclical resurgence of mercantilist policies, connected with the crisis of British world hegemony and with intensifying tendencies toward overproduction. If they had been treated in this way, the retreat into political economy would have merely implied a recognition of the fact that the path leading the capitalist world-economy to the ideal–typical asymptote envisaged in Marx's critique of political economy was characterized by cycles and discontinuities that could increase, even for relatively long periods, the distance separating historical circumstances from such an asymptote. Instead, monopoly capitalism and imperialism were theorized as the highest and final stage of the capitalist world-system, that is, as themselves representing the asymptote. In this way, Marxism as canonized by Lenin has come to be perversely identified as (and therefore with) political economy.

Weber's writings on processes of group formation in the modern world are undoubtedly among the most extensive available. For present purposes we limit our attention to his highly influential contrast of classes and status-groups (*Stände*). The contrasted categories were at once an advance over the class analysis projected by Marx and a retreat from it. They were an advance because of the juxtaposition of status-group formation to class formation. They were a retreat because of the restriction of the processes, and the resulting elemental forms of social structure, to existent "political communities" (which "under modern conditions . . . are 'states'") (1968: 904). We require in our work on modern social change the kind of juxtaposition Weber constructed. But in order to have it, we need to free it from the assumptions he made. And, in order to do that, we need to examine those assumptions.

Modern sociology would have us believe that Weber wrote an essay on class, status, and party. He did nothing of the sort. It would furthermore have us believe that he juxtaposed class and status-group as two separate dimensions of something called stratification in modern societies, both in turn separate from the state (construed as the realm of "parties"), which he also did not do. We then must first set to one side these imposed readings in order to see what Weber did do, and so allow ourselves to examine the assumptions he did make.

This preliminary exercise can fortunately be quite brief. In the Roth-Wittich edition of *Economy and Society* (Weber, 1968), Chapter IX in Part Two is entitled "Political Communities." This chapter is provided with six sections, each titled, the sixth of which is entitled, "The distribution of power within the political community," and subtitled, "class, status, party." It is this section of this chapter that appears in Hans Gerth and Wright Mills, *Essays from Max Weber* (1946) as itself a "chapter" (there, Chapter VII) with its subtitle, "class, status, party," as its full title. As someone once said, much may be lost in translation.[1]

For Weber in Chapter IX of *Economy and Society*, there were two and only two possible basic ways for the distribution of power in political communities (that is, in the modern world, *states*) to be structured: it can be either class-structured or status-group-structured. For "power" (undifferentiated here) to be class-structured, the factual distribution of goods and services within the political community or state in question must be market-organized. If so, or in so far as it is so, the distribution of life chances among the members of the political community (and others in its territory) is determined by their relative position ("class situation") in the organizing complex of market relations, the basic categories of which are "property" and "lack of property." Alternatively, for "power" to be status-group-structured, the factual distribution of goods and services within the political community or state in question must be prestige-organized. If so, or in so far it is so, the distribution of life chances among the members of the political community (and others) is determined by their membership ("status situation") in the organizing complex

---

1. Weber scholars will know that most headings in the Roth-Wittich edition were provided not by Weber but by the editors of the writings combined to form *Economy and Society*. The key sentences from the section under discussion are for present purposes two:

The structure of every legal order directly influences the distribution of power, economic or otherwise, within its respective [political] community (1968: 926).

Now: "classes", "status groups", and "parties" are phenomena of the distribution of power within a [political] community (1968: 927).

of honorifically ranked communal groups, the basic categories of which are "positively esteemed" and "negatively esteemed."

While depicted as if positively different, a class-structured distribution of power within a political community differs from a status-group-structured distribution only in one governing respect, namely, whether the distribution of goods and services is effected through market relations (= "class-structured") or instead through non-market relations (= "status-group-structured"), that is, residually.[2] The two stated elemental ways in which a given political community may be socially structured, then, were for Weber central categories to use in tracing historically the rise of the market — that is, the historical displacement by market relations of any and all other kinds of social relations through which the "factors" of production are recurrently brought together, the resulting products are "circulated," the embodied surpluses are "realized" and appropriated, and the material means of subsistence are "distributed." To the extent that relations among status-groups organize and mediate these flows, the market (the complex of market relations) does not, and classes in his terms are unformed. To the extent that the market organizes the flows, status-group relations do not, and status-groups are unformed (or better, "eroded," since the historical transformation from feudalism to capitalism in Europe underpins the contrast).

Still, even given the one-dimensionality of the distinction, it retained in its elaboration a matter of central importance, that of *an sich/für sich* derived from Marx. Weber made use of it in a particular manner. Classes in relation to one another, in a given political community, are *an sich* by definition but not thereby *für sich*. Here he followed quite

---

2. It is not until Polanyi (in *The Great Transformation* [1957] and subsequent writings) gave positive content to "non-market forms of integration" that this residual category began to receive systematic conceptual elaboration.

unambiguously the pre-Marx conventional political economy, seeing immediate class interests as given by market position and hence as theoretically indeterminate, so far as collective action is concerned, whether it be directly in relation to other classes or indirectly through their relation to the apparatus of the political community (state). Theoretically, something in addition to class interests must be introduced if one is to account for (continuous) collective class action and so therefore for its absence. In contrast, status-groups in relation to one another are by definition *groups*, definitionally endowed with the capacity to act collectively in relation to one another and to act on their respective behalfs in relation to the state.

The definitional difference was not arbitrary for Weber. A political community entails by construction "value systems" (1968: 902), in accordance with which its constituent elements have more or less legitimacy, prestige, and so on, in comparison with one another, and with reference to which they have more or less pride, solidarity, or capacity to act collectively in relation with one another. A status-group structuring of the distribution of power, because the constituent groups are arrayed honorifically by rank, confers on each more or less prestige and pride, and through that, the solidarity and capacity to act collectively in relation to one another. A class structuring of this distribution of power, in contrast, because of the market principle — which, in its operations for Weber, either eliminates all considerations of honor from its relations or is constrained in its working by them — provides its constituent classes with no necessary solidarity in their relations with one another, and hence no necessary capacity for collective action in or on these relations. In short, and to go a bit beyond Weber in this summary, status-groups are constituents of and thereby carriers of a moral order, in Durkheim's sense. Classes are not; if they become so, it is by virtue of processes fundamental but different from, and not entailed in, those that constitute them as classes in relation to one another.[3]

All of this is subject to the very strict proviso that we are examining the possible social structurings of the distribution of power *within* a constituted political community, a state under modern conditions. Weber himself, however, earlier opened up the possibility of freeing the contrasted categories of class and status-group from this highly constraining premise of their construction. In Section Three, headed "Power, prestige and the 'Great Powers,'" he asserted that states in relation to one another "may pretend to a special 'prestige,' and their pretensions may influence" the conduct of their relations with one another. "Experience teaches," he continues,

> that claims to prestige have always played into the origins of wars. Their part is difficult to gauge; it cannot be determined in general, but it is very obvious. The realm of "honor," which is comparable to the "status order" *within* a social structure, pertains also to the *interrelations of* political structures (1968: 911; italics added).

But extending the scope of stratifying processes,[4] so that

---

3. Weber's one theoretical claim in this section, Section Six of the Chapter "Political Communities," reads thus:

As to the general economic conditions making for the predominance of stratification by status, only the following can be said. When the bases of the acquisition and distribution of goods are relatively stable, stratification by status is favored. Every technological repercussion and economic transformation threatens stratification by status and pushes the class situation into the foreground. Epochs and countries in which the naked class situation is of predominant significance are regularly the periods of technical and economic transformations. And every slowing down of the change in economic stratification leads, in due course, to the growth of status structures and makes for resuscitation of the important role of social honor (1968: 938).

4. We have departed from Weber's use of "stratification." For a provisional and programmatic formulation of the concept, "stratifying processes," see Hopkins & Wallerstein (1981).

their operation within the interstate system of the world-economy is "comparable" to their suggested operation within one of its units (a political community, whether sovereign state or colony), runs into deeply serious difficulties. An illustration of this claim is all that time and space here permit.

Weber, in a "fragment" on "The Market" (Chapter VII of Part Two in the Roth-Wittich edition [1968: 635–40]), distinguished appropriately and sharply between two fundamentally different kinds of "monopolies" encountered within a given political community. On the one side are "the monopolies of status-groups [which] excluded from their field of action the mechanism of the market." On the other side are the "capitalistic monopolies which are acquired in the market through the power of property." The difference is elliptically specified: "The beneficiary of a monopoly by a status-group restricts, and maintains his power against, the market, while the rational–economic monopolist rules through the market" (1968: 639). The general difficulty we alluded to may be exemplified as follows. Supposing that, among our interrelated and honor-oriented states, the government of one creates a "monopoly" within its borders for its few local (national) producers of, say, automobiles, by so raising the import duties on automobiles produced elsewhere in the world that they are no longer price-competitive. They are, as is said, "priced out of the market," which amounts to saying that the government in question has restricted, and maintained its power against, the world market for automobiles. Do we construe that situation as comparable on the world scene to a status-group monopoly within a political community, or to a class-formed capitalistic monopoly? Or is it a bit of both — class-like because of the rational appropriation of profit opportunities by the automobile firms who persuaded the government to introduce the restrictions; and status-group-like because of the sentiments of national pride and prestige marshalled in support of and generated by the policy?

We suspect the latter. But if we are right, Weber's sharply etched structural distinction, between class-structured and status-group-structured distributions of power within political communities, becomes a fused concept when put to use in the examination of processes of group-formation in the modern world-system. And we shall have to ground anew processes of class-formation and processes of status-group-formation, in order to see them on occasion as fused and reinforcing sets of processes rather than being restricted by their original and careful formulation as necessarily diametrically opposed in their operation.

The intellectual pressure to reify groups, to presume their permanency and longevity, is difficult to resist. For one thing, most self-conscious groups argue as part of their legitimizing ideology not merely their preeminence (in one way or another) but their temporal priority over competing groups. Groups that are self-conscious, that seem to act collectively in significant ways, often seem very solid and very resilient. We too often lose from sight the degree to which this solidarity, this reality, is itself the product of the group's activities in relations with others, activities that in turn are made possible by and have a direct impact upon the rest of social reality. The very activities of groups in relation to one another serve to change each group substantially and substantively, and in particular to change their respective boundaries and their distinguishing and defining characteristics.

Permit us to suggest an analogy. If one has a wheel of mottled colors, one that includes the whole range of the color spectrum, and if one spins the wheel, it will appear more and more like a solid white mass as the speed increases. There comes a point of speed where it is impossible to see the wheel as other than pure white. If, however, the wheel slows down, the white will dissolve into its component separate colors. So it is with groups, even (and perhaps especially) those most central of institutional structures of the modern world-system — the states, the classes, the nations, and/or ethnic groups.[5] Seen in long historical time and broad world space, they fade into one another, becoming only "groups." Seen in short historical time and narrow world space, they become clearly defined and so form distinctive "structures."

The distinction between classes *an sich* and classes *für sich* is helpful insofar as it recognizes that the self-consciousness of classes (and other groups) is not a constant but a variable. We must, however, draw on Marx and Weber one step further and recognize with them that the very existence of particular historical groups in relation to one another is not given but is also a variable. It may be objected that no one ever assumed that a class or an ethnic group *always* existed, and that everyone knows that for every group there is of course a moment of its coming into existence (however difficult this may be to specify). But this is not the point we are making.

At some moment of historical time the bourgeoisie (the world bourgeoisie or a local version in a given area, or of a given people), the Brahmin caste, the Hungarian nation, and the religious community of Buddhists all came (or evolved) into existence. Are we to assume that each just continued to exist from that point on? We are contending that there is a sense in which all these groups are in fact constantly being recreated such that over time we have genuinely new wine in old bottles, and that the emphasis on the continuity and primordiality of the group's existence, though it maybe of considerable ideological value to its members as such, is of very little analytic value to us as observers. The transition from feudalism to capitalism

---

5. This theme is developed in Wallerstein (1980).

cannot be explained by the struggle of classes that came into real current existence only *as the result of* that transition. Civil war in Lebanon cannot be explained by the struggle of religious groups who have come into real *current existence* largely as a result of that civil war.

What intelligent analysis therefore requires is that we uncover the processes by which groups (and institutions) are constantly recreated, remoulded, and eliminated in the ongoing operations of the capitalist world-economy, which is an actual social system that came into historical existence primarily in Europe in the "long" sixteenth century, and which subsequently has been expanded in space so that it now includes all other geographical areas of the globe. The relational concept and, therefore, the actual structures of classes and ethnic groups have been dependent on the creation of the modern states. The states are the key political units of the world-economy, units that have been defined by and circumscribed by their location in the interstate system. And this system has served as the evolving political superstructure of the world-economy.

In the original loci of the capitalist world-economy, the birth of diplomacy, of so-called international law, and of state-building ideologies (such as absolutism) all coincide with the early functioning of the world-economy. Of course, these states rapidly found themselves in a hierarchical network of unequal strength. As new areas became incorporated into this capitalist world-economy, the existing political structures of such areas were commonly reshaped in quite fundamental ways (including even the definition of their territorial and "ethnic" or national boundaries) so that they could play their expected roles in the relational network of the interstate system. These states had to be too weak to interfere with the flow of the factors of production across their boundaries, and therefore with the peripheralization of their production processes. Hence, in some cases, pre-existing political structures had to be "weakened." But the states also had to be *strong* enough to ensure the very same flow, the same peripheralization. Hence, in other cases, pre-existing political structures had to be "strengthened." But weakened or strengthened, these recreated or entirely newly created incorporated states ended up as state structures that were weak relative to the states specializing in core production processes within the world-economy.

The classes and the ethnic/national groups or groupings that began to crystallize were crystallized, so to speak, from three directions. They defined themselves primarily in relation to these state structures that commanded the largest amount of armed force and access to economic possibilities, either through the direct distribution of ever-increasing tax income or through the creation of structured possibilities of preferential access to the market (including training). They were defined by those in the centers of these structures (and in the centers of the world-system as a whole). And they were perceived by competitive groups in their relational setting.

Three kinds of groups emerged in relation to these state structures — class, national, and ethnic groups. While classes *an sich* developed in terms of the relation of households to the real social economy, which in this case was a capitalist *world*-economy, a class *für sich* is a group that makes conscious claims of class membership, which is a claim to a place in a particular political order. Such a class could therefore only grow up in relation to a given political entity. When E.P. Thompson (1964) writes about the making of the English working class, he is writing about the conditions under which urban proletarians within a jurisdiction called "England" came to think of themselves as English workers and to act politically in this capacity. The class "made" itself, as he emphasizes, not only by the evolution of objective economic and social conditions, but by the ways in which some (many) people reacted to these conditions.

Of course, the exent to which there emerged an English rather than a British working class already indicated that a key political choice had been made. The Irish workers, for example, were thereby defined as a different group. Thus, the construction of a "class" was *ipso facto* part of the construction of at least two "nationalities," the English and the Irish. Nor did this particular story stop there. For we are still seeing today the later consequences of these early developments. Protestant urban proletarians in Northern Ireland do not today think of themselves as "Irish." Instead they call themselves "Protestants," or "Ulstermen," or (least likely) "Britons," or even all three. It is clear that, in reality, to be a "Protestant" and to be an "Ulsterman" is in this situation virtually synonymous; to be a "Catholic" and to be "Irish" is also synonymous. To be sure, there are Protestants, and even Jews resident in Dublin who think of themselves as Irish. This doesn't mitigate the meaning of the religious terms in Northern Ireland.

If now some political organization comes along and insists on banning the use of religious terminology in favor, let us say, of the exclusive use of class terminology, such a group is arguing in favor of a particular political resolution of the conflict. Were such a group to succeed, the reality of the religious groups as social entities might rapidly recede in Northern Ireland, as they have in many other areas of the world. An example would be Switzerland, where people primarily identify as members of linguistic groups and only in a minor way as members of religious groups.

Is there an Indian bourgeoisie? This is not a question of essences, but of existential reality. It is a political question that divides Indian entrepreneurs among themselves. To the extent that we can say that there exists an Indian bourgeoisie, as opposed to merely members of the world bourgeoisie who happen to hold Indian passports, it is because there is a belief on the part of these bourgeois that the Indian state apparatus has or could have an important role in assuring their "class" interests vis-à-vis both workers in India and bourgeois in other areas of the world.

The whole line between classes as they are constructed and status-groups of every variety is far more fluid and blurred than the classic presumption of an antinomy between class and status-group has indicated. It is in fact very hard to know when we are dealing primarily with the one rather than with the other. This is especially true when political conflict becomes acute, and this is one of the reasons why the lines between social movements and national movements have become increasingly difficult to disentangle and are perhaps unimportant to discern.

Furthermore, even among traditionally defined status-groups, it is not sure that it is very useful to distinguish "nations" from other kinds of "ethnic groups." A "nation" seems to be nothing but a political claim that the boundaries of a state should coincide with those of a given "ethnic group." This is used to justify either secessionist movements or unification movements. In point of fact, if we were to use a strict definition of the concept "nation," we should be hard-pressed to find even one "nation-state" in the entire world-system. This indicates that "nation" is more the description of an aspiration, or of a tendency, than of an existing phenomenon. Whenever the political claim (and/or definition by others) is less than that of state sovereignty, we tend to call this group an "ethnic group," whatever the basis of the claim, be it common language, common religion, common skin color, or fictive common ancestry.

The actual history of the construction (reconstruction, remolding, destruction) of classes, nations, and ethnic groups — including the pressure both of "external" groups to create these groups and of the "internal" desire of putative groups to create themselves — is a history of the constant rise and fall of the intensity of these political claims in cultural clothing. There is no evidence that, over the several hundred years of the existence of the capitalist world-economy, one particular genre of claim has grown at the expense of others; each genre seems to have held its own. It would seem, therefore, that assertions about primordiality are in fact ideological. This is not to say that there has not been systemic development. For example, nothing herein argued is inconsistent with the proposition that there has been growing class polarization in the capitalist world-economy. But such a proposition would be referring to classes *an sich*, that is, at the level of the real social economy, the capitalist world-economy. Rather, this analysis should be seen as an argument that group formations (solidarities) are processes of the capitalist world-economy, and are among the central underlying forms of the more narrowly manifest efforts at political organization.

In recent years, social scientists of various intellectual schools have begun to return to Marx's critique of political economy, but in ways that go beyond the mechanical usages of class analysis that formed the ideology of the Second and Third Internationals and beyond the equally mechanical concept of primordial status-groups that dominated the developmentalist ideology of US-dominated world social science in the 1950s and 1960s.

On the one hand, in the era of US hegemony (roughly 1945–70), the unity of the world market analytically presupposed by Marx (when he observed an era of British hegemony) and which was thought to have disappeared in the late nineteenth century, was in fact progressively reconstituted. The so-called transnationals sought to operate with minimal constraint by state-political apparatuses. Though the concentration of capital increased even further, its transnational expansion out of the American core became a major factor in the intensification of world market competition and in the consolidation of the unity of the world market. In this context the role played by states changed radically, though not everywhere to the same extent. Particularly outside of the Communist world, the emphasis in their action changed from territorial expansion and restriction of inter-enterprise competition within and across national/imperial boundaries, to strengthening the competitive edge of their territories as locales of production and to sustaining the transnational expansion of their respective national capitals. They thereby contributed to the enhancement of the density and connectedness of world-economic networks that, in turn, undermined their ability to influence/control economic activity even within their own borders.

On the other hand, the antisystemic movements have more and more taken on the clothing of "national-liberation movements," claiming the double legitimacy of nationalist anti-imperialism and proletarian anti-capitalism. This has given them great strength as mobilizing movements. But, insofar as they have come to power in specific state structures operating within the interstate system, they have been caught in the constraints of this system that has led, among other things, to conflicts within and among such "post-revolutionary" states.

A cogent analysis of existing trends within the world-system requires both a return to basics, in terms of an analysis of the operational mechanisms of capitalism as a mode of production, and a reconceptualization of the operational mechanisms of the social groups (that are formed, are reformed, and of course also disappear) that compete and conflict within this capitalist world-economy, as it continues to evolve and to transform itself.

2

Dilemmas of Antisystemic Movements

Opposition to oppression is coterminous with the existence of hierarchical social systems. Opposition is permanent, but for the most part latent. The oppressed are too weak — politically, economically, and ideologically — to manifest their opposition constantly. However, as we know, when oppression becomes particularly acute, or expectations particularly deceived, or the power of the ruling stratum falters, people have risen up in an almost spontaneous manner to cry halt. This has taken the form of revolts, of riots, of flight.

The multiple forms of human rebellion have for the most part been only partially efficacious at best. Sometimes they have forced the oppressors to reduce the pressure or the exploitation. But sometimes they have failed utterly to do so. However, one continuing sociological characteristic of these rebellions of the oppressed has been their "spontaneous," short-term character. They have come and they have gone, having such effect as they did. When the next such rebellion came, it normally had little explicit relationship with the previous one. Indeed, this has been one of the great strengths of the world's ruling strata throughout history — the noncontinuity of rebellion.

In the early history of the capitalist world-economy, the situation remained more or less the same as it had always been in this regard. Rebellions were many, scattered, discrete, momentary, and only partially efficacious at best. One of the contradictions, however, of capitalism as a system is that the very integrating tendencies that have been one of its defining characteristics have had an impact on the form of antisystemic activity.

Somewhere in the middle of the nineteenth century — 1848 is as good a symbolic date as any — there came to be a sociological innovation of profound significance for the politics of the capitalist world-economy. Groups of persons involved in antisystemic activity began to create a new institution: the continuing organization with members, officers, and specific political objectives (both long-run and short-term).

Such organized antisystemic movements had never existed before. One might argue that various religious sects had performed analogous roles with an analogous organization, but the long-run objectives of the religious sects were by definition otherworldly. The antisystemic organizations that came into existence in the nineteenth century were preeminently political, not religious — that is, they focused on the structures of "this world."

Social Movements and National Movements

In the course of the nineteenth century, two principal varieties of antisystemic movements emerged — what came to be called respectively the "social movement" and the "national movement." The major difference between them lay in their definition of the problem. The social movement defined the oppression as that of employers over wage earners, the bourgeoisie over the proletariat. The ideals of the French Revolution — liberty, equality, and fraternity —

could be realized, they felt, by replacing capitalism with socialism. The national movement, on the other hand, defined the oppression as that of one ethno-national group over another. The ideals could be realized by giving the oppressed group equal juridical status with the oppressing group by the creation of parallel (and usually separate) structures.

There has been a long discussion, within the movements and among scholars, about the differences between these two kinds of movement. No doubt they have differed both in their definitions of the problem and in the social bases of their support. In many places and at many times, the two varieties of movement felt they were in direct competition with each other for the loyalty of populations. Less frequently in the nineteenth century, but sometimes, the two varieties of movement found enough tactical congruence to work together politically.

The traditional emphasis on the differences of the two varieties of movement has distracted our attention from some fundamental similarities. Both kinds of movement, after considerable internal debate, created formal organizations. As such, these organizations had to evolve a basic strategy to transform their immediate world in the direction in which they wished it to go. In both cases, the analysis was identical. The key political structure of the modern world they each saw to be the state. If these movements were to change anything, they had to control a state apparatus, which pragmatically meant "their" state apparatus. Consequently, the primary objective had to be obtaining state power.

For the social movement, this meant that, despite the internationalism of their ideology — "workers of the world, unite!" — the organizations they created had to be national in structure. And the objective of these organizations had to be the coming to power of the movement *in that state.* Similarly, for the national movement, the objective came to

be state power in a particular state. To be sure, the jurisdiction of this state was by definition what the national
movement was about. Sometimes such a movement sought
the creation of an entirely new state, either by secession or
by merger, but in other cases this "new state" might have
already existed in the form of a colonial or a regional
administrative entity.

The fact that the two varieties of movement defined the
same strategic objective accounts for their sense of rivalry
with each other, particularly when a workers' movement
sought to obtain power in an entity out of which a given
national movement was seeking to detach a zone in order to
create a new state.

The parallel objectives — obtaining state power — led to
a parallel internal debate on the mode of obtaining state
power, which might be defined in polar terms as the legal
path of political persuasion versus the illegal path of insurrectionary force. This has often been called reform versus
revolution, but these two terms have become so overlaid
with polemic and confusion that today they obscure more
than they aid analysis.

It should be noted that in the case of the social movement, this internal debate culminated during the period
between the First and Second World Wars in the existence
of two rival and fiercely competitive Internationals, the
Second and the Third, also known as the conflict between
Social Democrats and Communists. Though both the
Second and Third Internationals asserted that they had the
same objective of socialism, that they were movements
based in the working class and on the left, and even (at least
for a while) that they assumed the same Marxist heritage,
they rapidly became vehemently opposed one to the other,
to the extent that their subsequent occasional political
convergences (the "popular fronts") have seemed at best
tactical and momentary. In some sense, this has remained
true right up to the present.

If one looks at the geography of the movements, one quickly notices a historical correlation. Social-democratic movements have become politically strong and have "come to power" (by electoral means, to be sure, and then in alternation with more conservative parties) almost only in the core states of the world-economy, but in virtually all of them. Communist parties, by contrast, have become politically strong primarily in a certain range of semiperipheral and peripheral zones, and have come to power (sometimes by insurrection, but sometimes as a result of military occupation by the USSR) only in these zones. The only Western countries in which Communist parties have been relatively strong for a long period of time are France, Italy, and Spain, and it should be noted that Italy and Spain might well be considered semiperipheral. In any case, the parties in these three states have long since shed any insurrectionary inclinations.

We are therefore in the 1980s faced with the following political history of the modern world. Social-democratic parties have in fact achieved their primary political objective, coming to power in a relatively large number of core states. Communist parties have in fact come to power in a significant number of semiperipheral and peripheral countries — concentrated geographically in a band that runs from Eastern Europe to East and Southeast Asia. And in the rest of the world, in many of the countries, nationalist — sometimes even "radical nationalist" or "national liberation" — movements have come to power. In short, seen from the vantage point of 1848, the success of the antisystemic movements has been very impressive indeed.

The Unfulfilled Revolution

How are we to appreciate the consequences? In gross terms, we can see two consequences that have moved in very different directions. On the one hand, these movements, taken collectively as a sort of "family" of movements, have become an increasingly consequential element in the politics of the world-system and have built upon their achievements. Later movements have profited from the successes of earlier movements by moral encouragement, example, lessons in political tactics, and direct assistance. Many concessions have been wrested from the world's ruling strata.

On the other hand, the coming to state power of all these movements has resulted in a very widespread sense of unfulfilled revolution. The questions have run like this. Have social-democratic parties achieved anything more than some redistribution to what are in fact "middle" strata located in core countries? Have Communist parties achieved anything more than some economic development for their countries? And even then, how much? And furthermore, has this not been primarily to benefit the so-called new class of a bureaucratic elite? Have nationalist movements achieved anything more than allowing the so-called comprador class a slightly larger slice of the world pie?

These are perhaps not the questions that ought to be asked, or the manner in which the issues should be posed. But in fact these are the questions that have been asked, and very widely. There is little doubt that the resulting skepticism has made deep inroads in the ranks of potential and even active supporters of the world's antisystemic movements. As this skepticism began to take hold, there were a number of ways in which it began to express itself in ideological and organizational terms.

The period after the Second World War was a period of great success for the historic antisystemic movements. Social democracy became firmly ensconced in the West. It is less that the social-democratic parties came to be seen as one of the alternating groups which could legitimately govern than that the main program of the social democrats, the welfare state, came to be accepted by even the conservative parties, if no doubt begrudgingly. After all, even Richard Nixon said: "We are all Keynesians now." Communist parties, of course, came to power in a whole series of states. And the post-1945 period saw one long process of decolonization, punctuated by some dramatic, politically important armed struggles, such as Vietnam, Algeria, and Nicaragua.

Nonetheless, by the 1960s, and even more by the 1970s, there began to occur a "break with the past" with the rise of a new kind of antisystemic movement (or movements within the movements) in world-regional locales as diverse as North America, Japan, Europe, China, and Mexico. The student, Black, and antiwar movements in the United States; the student movements in Japan and Mexico; the labor and student movements in Europe; the Cultural Revolution in China; and as of the 1970s the women's movements; did not have identical roots or even common effects. Each one was located in political and economic processes shaped by the particular and different histories, and by the different positions in the world-system of the locales in which they arose and worked themselves out. Yet, by world-historical standards, they occurred in the same period and, moreover, they shared some common ideological themes that clearly set them apart from earlier varieties of antisystemic movements.

Their almost simultaneous occurrence can largely be traced to the fact that the movements of the late 1960s were precipitated by a common catalyst: the escalation of the anti-imperialist war in Vietnam. This escalation posed an immediate threat to the established patterns of life, and to the very lives not only of the Vietnamese but of American youth as well, and the war posed a clear threat to the security of the Chinese people. As for European youth and workers, while no immediate threat was posed to their lives and security, the indirect effects of the escalation (world monetary crisis, intensification of market competition, and so on) and the ideological spill-overs from the movements in the United States, from the Cultural Revolution in China, and from the struggle of the Vietnamese people soon provided enough reasons and rationalizations for rebellion.

Taken together, all these movements and their Vietnamese epicenter were important in disclosing a basic asymmetry in the power of systemic and antisystemic forces on a world scale. The asymmetry was most dramatically exemplified on the battlefields themselves. Following the precedent of the Chinese war of national liberation, the Vietnamese showed how a national-liberation movement could, by shifting the confrontation with conventional armies onto nonconventional terrains (as in guerrilla warfare), erode and eventually disintegrate the social, political, and military position of cumbersome imperial forces. From this point of view, the other movements (particularly the US antiwar movement) were part and parcel of this asymmetrical relation: to different degrees and in different ways, they showed how the shift of the confrontation between systemic and antisystemic forces onto nonconventional terrain was strengthening the latter and hampering/paralyzing the former.

The outcome and implications of the combined and uneven development of the antisystemic movements of the 1960s and 1970s must be assessed at different levels. Locally, the Vietnam war had a very "conventional" outcome: the coming to state power of a "classical" antisystemic movement, and the subsequent strengthening of the bureaucratic structure of this state. Assessed from this angle, at the national level the outcome of the Vietnamese national-liberation movement did not differ significantly from the earlier kinds of antisystemic movements (national and social). Globally, however, the Vietnam war was a turning point in disclosing the limits of military actions in coercing the periphery into a hierarchical world order.

These limits and their recognition were the outcome not only of the confrontation on the battlefields but also, and possibly to a greater degree, of the movements unleashed elsewhere in the world-system. It was the nature of these other movements that most clearly marked a departure from, and a counterposition to, earlier patterns of anti-systemic movements. To varying degrees, the Cultural Revolution in China, the student movements in the West, Japan, and Mexico, and the "autonomist" workers' movements in Europe took as one of their themes the limits and dangers of the establishment and consolidation of bureaucratic structures by the movements themselves, and this was new.

The Cultural Revolution was largely directed against the bureaucratic power of the Communist Party and, whatever its failures from other points of view, its main achievement has been precisely to have prevented, or at least slowed down, the consolidation of party bureaucratic power in China. The student and youth movements that cropped up in the most diverse contexts were generally directed not only against the various bureaucratic powers that tried to curb and repress them (states, universities, parties) but also against all attempts to channel them toward the formation of new, and the strengthening of old, bureaucratic organizations. Although the new workers' movements generally ended up by strengthening bureaucratic organizations (mostly unions), nonetheless the protagonists of these "new" movements showed an unprecedented awareness of the fact that bureaucratic organizations such as unions were bound to develop interests of their own that might differ in important respects from those of the workers they claimed to represent. What this meant, concretely, was that the instrumental attitude of unions and parties vis-à-vis the movement was matched and countered to an unprecedented extent by an instrumental attitude on the part of the movement vis-à-vis unions and parties.

The anti-bureaucratic thrust of the movements of the

1960s and early 1970s can be traced to three main tendencies: the tremendous widening and deepening of the power of bureaucratic organizations as a result of the previous wave of antisystemic movements; the decreasing capabilities of such organizations to fulfill the expectations on which their emergence and expansion had been based; and the increasing efficacy of direct forms of action, that is, forms unmediated by bureaucratic organizations. On the first two tendencies, nothing needs to be added to what has already been said concerning the successes and limits of the earlier movements, except to point out that the reactivation of market competition under US hegemony since the Second World War had further tightened the world-economy constraints within which states acted.

As for the increasing efficacy of direct forms of action, the tendency concerns mainly the labor movement and was rooted in the joint impact of two key trends of the world-economy: the trend toward an increasing commodification of labor power and the trend toward increasing division of labor and mechanization. In the previous stage, labor movements came to rely on permanent bureaucratic organizations aiming at the seizure or control of state power for two main reasons. First, these labor movements were largely at the beginning the expression of artisans and craft workers who had been or were about to be proletarianized but whose bargaining power vis-à-vis employers still depended on their craft skills. As a consequence, these workers had an overwhelming interest in restricting the supply of, and expanding the demand for, their skills. This, in turn, required trade-union organizations oriented to the preservation of craft-work roles in the labor process on the one hand, and to control over the acquisition of craft skills on the other. Like all organizations that attempt to reproduce "artificially" (that is, in opposition to historical tendencies) a scarcity that affords monopolistic quasi-rents, these craft or craft-oriented unions ultimately depended for their success on the ability to use state power to restrain employers from profiting from the operations of the market. The artificial (that is, nonmarket) restraints were twofold: state rules about workers' pay and conditions; state legitimation of unionization and collective bargaining.

The second and more important reason for the previous reliance of labor movements on permanent bureaucratic organizations aiming at state power was related to the question of alliances and hegemony. In most national locales, the struggle between labor and capital took place in a context characterized by the existence of wide strata of peasants and middle classes which could be mobilized politically to support anti-labor state policies, and economically to enhance competition within the ranks of labor. Under these circumstances labor could obtain long-term victories only by neutralizing or winning over to its side significant fractions of these strata. And this could not be achieved through spontaneous and direct action, which often had the effect of alienating the strata in question. Rather, it required a political platform that would appeal to peasants and the middle strata, and an organization that would elaborate and propagandize that platform.

By the 1960s radical changes had occurred from both points of view, in core regions and in many semiperipheral countries. The great advances in the technical division of labor and in mechanization of the interwar and postwar years had destroyed or peripheralized in the labor process the craft skills on which labor's organized power had previously rested. At the same time, these very advances had endowed labor with a new power: the power to inflict large losses on capital by disrupting a highly integrated and mechanized labor process. In exercising this power, labor was far less dependent on an organization external to the workplace (as trade unions generally were), since what really mattered was the capacity to exploit the interdependencies and networks created by capital itself in the workplace.

Moreover, the increased commodification of labor had depleted the locally available strata of peasants that could be effectively and competitively mobilized to undermine the political and economic power of labor. As for the middle strata, the unprecedented spread and radicalism of the student movements were symptoms of the deepening commodification of the labor power of these strata, and of the greater difficulties of mobilizing them against the labor movement. (This process was reflected in an extensive literature of the 1960s on the "new working class.") It follows that the problem of alliances and hegemony was less central than in the past and that, as a consequence, labor's dependence on permanent bureaucratic organizations for the success of its struggles was further reduced.

As we have seen, for many persons the conclusion to be drawn from this analysis is that the antisystemic movements have "failed" or, even worse, were "co-opted." The change from "capitalist state" to "socialist state," for many who think in these terms, has not had the transforming effects on world history — the reconstituting of trajectories of growth — that they had believed it would have. And the change from colony to state, whether by revolution or by negotiation, has lacked not only the world-historical effects but also, in most instances, even the internal redistribution of well-being so prominent in the programs of these movements. Social democracy has succeeded no better. Everywhere it finds its occupancy of state power merely a mediating presence — one constrained by the processes of accumulation on a world scale and by the twin requirements of governments: burying the dead and caring for the wounded, whether people or property. To the chagrin of some, the applause of others, the one coordinated effort toward a world revolution, the Comintern/Cominform, collapsed completely under the disintegrating weight of continuing state formation at all the locations of its operations — its historical center, its loci of subsequent success, its other national arenas of strength, its points of marginal presence. Without exception, all current Communist parties are concerned first with domestic conditions and only secondarily if at all with world revolution.

The Transformed Historical Ground

We, on the other hand, contend, as we said, that from the vantage point of 1848 the success of the antisystemic movements has been very impressive indeed. Moreover, that success does not dim in the least when viewed from the vantage point of today. Rather the opposite. For without such an appreciation, one cannot understand where the nonconventional terrain opened up by the most recent forms of antisystemic movement has come from historically and where therefore the movements seem likely to go in the historical future.

At the same time, however, the antisystemic movements are of course not the only agencies to have altered the ground on which and through which current and future movements must continually form and operate. Those they would destroy — the organizing agencies of the accumulation process — have also been at work, owing partly to an "inner logic," partly to the very successes of the movements and hence to the continually transformed historical ground which that "logic" has as its field of operation and contradiction. Above all, the ongoing structural transformation of the capitalist world-economy has in effect opened up the locations in its overall operation where the process of class struggle is proving formative of the sides of conflict, and polarizing in the relations so formed.

In the course of the twentieth century, indeed defining it, a massive sea-change has been occurring in the social relations of accumulation. In a sentence, the relational networks forming the trunk lines of the circuits of capital have been so structurally transformed that the very work-ings of the accumulation process appear to be historically altered. It is this ongoing transformation that has continu-ally remade the relational conditions both of the organizing agencies of accumulation (by definition) and of those in fundamental struggle with them, the antisystemic move-ments; and so have continually remade as well the relational character of the struggle itself and hence the nature of the movements defined by it. To retrace the steps: the life cycles of the various movements have been a part of and have helped to form the structural shift; hence the relational struggles defining the movements as antisystemic; hence the movements themselves and the trajectories that make them antisystemic. We depict the ongoing trans-formation here by outlining three of its faces in the form of structural trends.

In one guise the transformation appears as simulta-neously an increasing "stateness" of the world's peoples (the number of "sovereign states" having more than tripled during the twentieth century) and an increasingly dense organization of the interstate system. Today virtually the whole of the globe's nearly five billion people are politically partitioned into the subject populations of the hundred-and-sixty or so states of an interstate system, which contains a large number of formal interstate organizations. This might be called the widening of stateness. The deepening of stateness is another matter. Here essentially we have in mind the growing "strength" of state agencies vis-à-vis local bodies (within or intersecting with the state's jurisdiction). Measures of this are of many sorts, from the voluminous expansion of laws and of agencies to enforce them, through central-government taxes as growing proportions of measured domestic or national product, to the structural expansion of kinds of state agency, the geographical spread of their locations of operation, and the growing proportion of the labor force formed by their employees. Moreover, like international airports around the world, and for analogous if deeper reasons, the organizational form of stateness (the complex array of hierarchies forming the apparatus of administration) has everywhere virtually the same anatomy, the differences from place to place being of the order of variations on a theme. They are variations that no doubt matter a great deal to the subjects of state power, but, world-historically, they are nonetheless only variations and not qualitative departures in form.

One final point should perhaps be noted here. Much has been made of the extent to which, following the accessions to power of social and/or national antisystemic movements, a marked increase in the structural "centralization" of the state has occurred, that is, a marked increase in what we're calling here the deepening of stateness. And, examining the trends in state formation within the jurisdictions severally, one at a time, one does see that. However, watching the overall trend in state formation in the modern world as a singular historical system over the course of the twentieth century, one would be hard put to attribute the overall trend to any such "internal" processes or, for that matter, even to the interrelated successes of the particular social and national movements construed collectively as but particular emanations of a singular complex historical process of the modern world-system. For even in locations where, seen in that way, the world-historical process has been manifestly weakest (the movements least apparently successful), the structural trend in state formation is no less apparent than elsewhere.

Of even more importance here, in some ways, is the still far greater growth in the density of the interstate system. Just using the simplest of assumptions, and reasoning purely formally from the fourfold increase in the number of states, there is a sixteenfold increase in their relations with one another. But that of course barely scratches the surface. The kinds of specialized relations among the states of the interstate system have expanded nearly as much as the kinds of internal state agency. Added to this there are over a dozen specialized United Nations agencies (in each of which most states are related as members) and a very large number of regional international organizations (such as OECD, OPEC, ASEAN, COMECON, NATO, OAU, and so on). If one goes beyond the existence of the voluminous set of interstate relations to the frequency with which they're activated, via meetings, postal mail, cable, telephone, and now, increasingly, electronic mail, the density of the *interstate* system's relational network today is probably several times greater than the comparable density of the official *intrastate* relational network of the most advanced and centrally administered country of a century ago (say, France).

One result is an enmeshing within each state's operations of the "internal" and "external" relational webs and processes to such an extent that the distinction itself, except perhaps for border crossings of people and goods, begins to lose substantive force (in contradiction to its nominal force, which is increased with every treaty signed, every package assessed for duty by customs, every postage stamp issued). Hence, to a degree and extent never envisioned by the successful social and national movements when they eventually gained state power, both what agencies of a state administer internally, and how they do this, is increasingly determined, to use a Weber pairing, not autonomously (as befits sovereignty) but heteronomously (as befits what?).

A second result, and one of no less importance to our subject — the current and future terrain on, through, and against which present and future antisystemic movements are and will be operating — is the degree to which virtually all interrelations among peoples in different state jurisdictions have become dimensions of their respective states' relations with one another. This is not just a matter of travelers obtaining passports and visas and passing through emigration and immigration authorities, or of packages having to be sent with export and import permits and be duly processed, and so forth. These interstate procedures, which daily re-announce the borders of the respective jurisdictions of each constituent state, are but mediations of the movement of people, goods, and capital, and have been practiced for a rather long time.

The "openness" or "closure" of a state's borders to such movements, however — we note parenthetically in passing — has always been less a matter of that state's policies "toward the world" than of its location in the hierarchical ordering inherent in the capitalist world-economy's interstate system. This location is determined not merely by academicians but by demonstrated or credible relational strengths, practical conditions effected by ruling classes. Rather it is a matter of the interstate system's appropriating all manner of direct and circuitous relations among people of different countries (state jurisdictions) — whether religious, scientific, commercial, artistic, financial, linguistic, civilizational, educational, literary, productive, problem-focused, historical, philosophical, *ad infinitum* — such that they all become, at the very least, mediated, more often actually organized, by the counterpart agencies of different states through their established or newly formed relations with one another. The effect is to subordinate the interrelations among the world's peoples not to *raisons d'état*, a practice with which all of us are all too familiar, but to *raisons du système d'états*, a practice with which most of us are all too unfamiliar.

There is, we should briefly note, a set of consequential historical contradictions being formed through this recreation of all varieties of social relations into networks within either inter- or intrastate frameworks. Many kinds of community — in the sense of communities of believers/ practitioners — form in a way "worlds" of their own in relation to, in distinction from, and often in conflict with all others; that is, those who are not of their community, who are nonbelievers or nonpractitioners, hence nonmembers. These are often large, encompassing worlds: the Islamic world; the scientific world; the African world (or, in the United States today, the Black world); the women's world; the workers' or proletarian world; and so forth. It is far from evident that such communities of consciousness can even persist, much less grow, within the structurally developing inter- and intrastate framework. The kind of contradiction noted here marks to an even greater extent the popular peace and environmental movements, but that is because they are perforce, in today's world, state-oriented; whereas the communities of consciousness we have in mind elaborate themselves independently of stateness (hence, however, in contradiction to it and to interstateness, rather than through them).

Division of Labor, Centralization of Capital

We have dwelt at length on but one face of the ongoing structural transformation of the capitalist world-economy; that seen through a focus on the plane of the interstate system and its constituent units, the states, and their relations with one another. We have done so for two reasons. One is the seemingly enduring disposition, on the part of historical social scientists, to carry forward — all evidence to the contrary notwithstanding — the liberal ideological distinction between "state" and "economy," or "state" and "market" in some versions, as if these were fundamental theoretical categories. The other is the equally prevalent, although apparently less impermeable, disposition to imagine — again, all evidence to the contrary notwithstanding — that the capitalist world-economy has evolved rather as an onion grows, from a core of small and local beginnings through successively larger rings until the outer peripheral skin is formed, all by virtue of, in this view, the self-expansion of capital through its increasing subordination of labor.

We turn now to much briefer observations on two more faces of this transformation. A second face is in the organization of the structuring of another plane of the capitalist world-economy's operation, the axial division of labor. This is the complex of interrelated production/transportation processes that is so ordered that the surplus-value created in the course of production and transportation is, historically, disproportionately appropriated at the organizing centers of the multiple and more-or-less lengthy chains or networks of dependent production processes. The relational patterns this ordering entails are thereby reproduced and, for additional reasons, their reproduction has cyclically deepened the differences in productive capacity between the organizing center or core portions of the axial division of labor and its increasingly peripheralized portions. In the twentieth century, the underlying transformation has effected some truly massive alterations in the constituent relations of the complex core–periphery axis and hence in the mapping of their respective global zones, the results of which — generally rendered as if the result of state policies — are broadly known. Of more immediate interest is the extraordinary growth in recent decades of a long-standing agency of the organizing center or core of the socialization of production (hence of labor) on a world scale; namely, what is currently called the multinational or transnational firm. In a sentence, many relations among materially dependent production processes that had been exchange relations — or, if newly formed, could have been under other conditions (and so of, or potentially of, market-organized networks of commodity flows) — became transformed into (or, if new, formed as) intrafirm relations. The elemental arrangement — centralizations of capital, in the form of firms, entrepreneurially organizing geographically extensive and technically complex (for the time) chains of related production operations — is hardly new. It was, after all, what distinguished the chartered merchant (sic!) companies of the seventeenth and eighteenth centuries from other capitalized operations. But in recent decades this "elemental arrangement" of the capitalist world-economy has been increasingly constituted on a scale, and in a form of both organization and production, that is historically original. The transnational corporations' reconstruction of the world-scale division and integration of labor processes fundamentally alters the historical possibilities of what are still referred to, and not yet even nostalgically, as "national economies."

A third face of the ongoing structural transformation we are sketchily addressing here shows itself, so to speak, in the massive centralization of capital of the postwar decades. Slowly, haltingly, but more and more definitely, the central agency of capitalist accumulation on a world scale, a world ruling class in formation, is *organizing* a relational structure for continually resolving the massive contradictions, increasingly apparent between the transnational corporations' control over, and hence responsibility for, the inter-relations *among* productive processes and the multiple states' control *over*, and hence responsibility for, the labor forces these production processes engage, more or less sporadically.

This structure being organized is basically a sort of replacement, at a "higher level" of course, for the late-lamented colonial empires, whose demise the national movements sought and the new hegemonic power, the United States, required. Through those arrangements, and such cousins of them as the Chinese concessions and the Ottoman capitulations, the axial division of labor had been furthered and, subject to the very system's structural cycles, assured. The twentieth century's thirty-years' war (1914–45), insofar as it was about those arrangements, resolved the question of hegemonic power (a United States versus Germany fight, it was then understood) but left for invention the means of its exercise and, with that, the perpetuation of both the axial division of labor and the necessary multiple sovereignties, through which the interstate system and hence the relations of hegemony operated.

The invention was a long time in coming and seems to have emerged fully only, as we said earlier, after the narrowness of the limits of great-power military force had finally been established by the Vietnamese for all to see. Crudely put, what seems to have been going on, by way of a structural replacement of the colonial empires, has been the simultaneous growth in massive centralizations of capital *and* a sort of deconcentration of capital (called deindustrialization in present core areas of the axial division of labor). The massive centralization has as its agencies quite small *ad hoc* steering committees of consortia, each composed of several hundred banks working in close relations both with central banks and with international agencies, notably the IBRD, and IMF, and the BIS. The centralization here is at the money point in the circuit of capital, and the borrowers are not directly capitalist entrepreneurs but are instead states, which in turn use the more-or-less encumbered credits to work with transnationals, operating with undistributed surpluses in various "development" projects, which, as they are realized materially, amount to what is called by some "Third World industrialization" and result in precisely the "deindustrialization" of previously core areas.

This face of the transformation does suggest reconsidering the theoretically presumed concatenation of centralization and concentration of capital. But even more it suggests reconceptualizing the *fundamental* nature of the accumulation process as it is framed through the idea of the circuits of capital. For when the indebted *states* run into trouble, one of the agencies of this arrangement, the IMF, steps forward with austerity plans, the gist and substance of which amount to lowering the costs, now internationally reckoned, of the daily and generational reproduction of the labor forces of (within?) each of the countries.

The arrangement is not *per se* historically new — one thinks of the Ottoman capitulations, for example — but it is far more massive and, as a structural array of processes of the world-system, far more frequent in occurrence and telling in its implications for the structuring of the accumulation process as such.

Together these three facets of the ongoing structural transformation of the modern world-system, all of which reveal, to a greater or lesser extent, the structural surround of the state power seized or occupied by antisystemic movements in the course of the twentieth century, and indicate the degree and kind of reconstitution of terrain with which present and future movements of a like sort have to contend. They indicate as well — though this is not here a central concern of ours — the anachronism of the contents we give to the concepts with which we commonly work. The dilemmas of the antisystemic movements are thus in some measure the unintended product of a sort of false consciousness on the part, not of toadies nor even of hairsplitters, but of the most engaged of the intelligentsia.

There remains a matter to end on here — to raise as a sort of coda — for nothing before has directly prefigured it. This is the ongoing transformation of communications networks. The *Communist Manifesto* observes: "And that union, to attain which the burghers of the Middle Ages, with their miserable highways, required centuries, the modern proletarians, thanks to railways, achieve in a few years." It is now nearly a century and a half since that was written. That sentence has lost none of its force. But it must be understood contemporarily. In the United States, in the 1960s, what effected the interrelation of the hundred-and-fifty or so Black demonstrations and the even more numerous public forms of the antiwar movement was television, which is why the commanding officer of the Grenada operation (Grenada: less than half the size in territory and people of an upstate New York county) correctly, from the US government's point of view, decreed there was to be no accompanying news coverage of the invasion. The kind of concern flagged in the *Manifesto*, the material means of unity among those geographically separate, remains central. The means themselves, and the very form of their materiality, have been fundamentally transformed. More and more antisystemic movements will find their own cohesion and coherence forged and destroyed by the newest of the means of mediating social relations.

Where then are we? We are massively, seriously in urgent need of reconstructing the strategy, perhaps the ideology, perhaps the organizational structure of the family of world antisystemic movements; if we are to cope effectively with the real dilemmas before which we are placed, as the "stateness" of states and the "capitalist" nature of capitalism grow at an incredible pace. We know this creates objective contradictions for the system as such and for the managers of the status quo. But it creates dilemmas for the antisystemic movements almost as grave. Thus we cannot count on the "automaticity" of progress; thus we cannot abandon critical analysis of our real historical alternatives.

3

The Liberation of Class Struggle?

Over the past few decades the relationship between national liberation and class conflict — between national-liberation struggles and proletarian-liberation struggles — has been presented in three broadly differing ways. The national struggle has been seen as a form, or even *the* form, of the class struggle on a world scale. The national struggle has been thought of as analogous to the class struggle because a revolutionary movement may organize the oppressed in each case and, with victory, effect fundamental changes in the world-scale social structuring of the accumulation process. The national struggle and the class struggle have also been seen as related historically, and so theoretically, but as different in kind because their historical trajectories differ, the one toward reproducing the capitalist world-economy by extending and deepening its interstate plane of operations, the other toward eliminating the capitalist world-economy by eliminating its defining bourgeois–proletarian relation. The first we think of as the ideological conception of the relation (between the national struggle and the class struggle); the second, as the political conception; the third, as the historical–theoretical conception.

We seek below to explicate these prefatory remarks in three ways. First, we shall sketch the rise and subsidence or quiescence of national liberation as a world-historical organizing — or better, reorganizing — force. Second, we shall seek to clarify the differences between, on the one hand the "vertical" relation and class categories formed by the class struggle, and on the other hand the "horizontal" relations of competition among and between "political" leaderships and "economic" leaderships that are often confounded with the "vertical" relations, both practically and theoretically. Third, we shall briefly outline the developmental processes that make the class struggle an increasingly overt and ramifying force for the transformation of the modern world-system, while at the same time operating in contradiction to its objectives by confining excessively its expression to changes in the relational structures of the interstate system.

The struggle for national liberation as we have come to know it has a long history. National liberation from what? Obviously, the answer is national liberation from the unequal relations among different zones of the modern world-system. This system has taken, as we know, the form of a capitalist world-economy, which has expanded in space over time, incorporated zones previously external to it, subordinated them (economically, politically, and culturally), and held them tightly within an integrated whole.

One of the fundamental ideological themes of all modern nationalism has been the struggle for equality — both the hypothetical equality of all members of the "nation" and the demand for equality with "outside" oppressor states/ groups. (Of course, this was only one of the themes. There has also been the theme of "uniqueness" which, under certain conditions, could be translated into a justification for the oppression of others.)

Egalitarian demands in the guise of nationalism are already in evidence in the nineteenth, even the late eighteenth, centuries. The struggle of White colonists for independence in the Americas, the Haitian revolution, the Spanish resistance to Napoleon, Mehemet Ali's effort to "modernize" Egypt, the "Springtime of the Nations" in 1848, Garibaldi and Kossuth, the founding of the Indian National Congress were all reflections of this global thrust.

But it is only in the twentieth century that we can see national-liberation movements as a major organizational phenomenon of the world-system. Even before the First World War, the political "revolutions" in Mexico, the Ottoman Empire, Persia, and China made it clear that, no sooner had the "expansion of Europe" reached its apogee (the last two decades of the nineteenth century), than the counterpressures immediately began to be significant.

The Russian Revolution of October 1917 was no doubt a turning point in the political history of the modern world-system. The Bolsheviks presented themselves as the protagonist of the working-class struggle for Communism, the outgrowth of the nineteenth-century "social movement" (at that time largely a European movement) of the proletariat against the bourgeoisie. This was no doubt the case. But from the outset, everyone remarked on the fact that this "first proletarian revolution" had taken place not in the most "advanced" capitalist country or countries (where the theory had predicted it would happen) but in a relatively "backward" zone.

Although much of the support for the revolution came from "proletarians" struggling against "bourgeois," surely one element of support for the Bolsheviks took the form of a drive for "national liberation." That this latter "nationalist" element was involved and was not always compatible with the other "class" element in the Bolshevik agenda was most poignantly and significantly reflected in the stormy career and eventual elimination of Sultan Galiev who called upon Bolshevik leaders to redirect their strategy from a concentration on Europe to a concentration on the "East." Lenin himself did try to bring together the world's "socialist" movements and the world's "national-liberation" movements in the Congress of Baku. Ever since, the cohabitation of these two "antisystemic" forces has remained both very real and very uneasy. In the last fifty years it has become more and more difficult to separate the two rhetorics (socialism and national liberation), and even to keep them organizationally separate (as the political histories of China and Vietnam both illustrate very well). This combination has been very efficacious. Nonetheless, the cohabitation of these two rhetorics, tendencies, forces, has been at best uneasy, at worst deeply obscuring of social reality.

At one level, since 1945, national-liberation movements have been magnificently successful. Almost all parts of the world that in 1945 were colonies of "metropolitan" states are today independent sovereign states, equal members of the United Nations. The process by which this occurred was threefold. On the one hand, in a certain number of states, there was a significant amount of organized armed struggle, which culminated in the coming to political power in the state of the movement that had led this armed struggle. In other states, merely the potential for such armed struggle by a movement, given the world context of the many armed struggles going on elsewhere, was enough to enable the movement to achieve power (usually by "electoral" means). Finally, in a third set of states, precisely in order to head off such movements, the metropolitan power arranged a transfer to power of some so-called moderate indigenous group (what the French called an "*indépendance octroyée*").

No doubt there are many instances in which the story falls in the interstices of this model. And no doubt, too, a few such struggles for the "transfer of power" are still going on, particularly in states that are already "sovereign" (South Africa, various parts of Central America, and so on). However, the bulk of the struggles for what might be called "formal" national liberation are now over. We are now able to look back upon what they have accomplished.

On the one hand, these struggles have accomplished very much. The arrogant and self-confident global racism involved in colonialism has disappeared or at least gone underground. The role of indigenous persons in the political decisions affecting the less powerful states of the world is considerably greater today than it was in 1945. The actual state policies of such countries have tended to reflect this "indigenization" of political decision-making.

On the other hand, the changes certainly have not been as great as the national-liberation movements had anticipated as of, say, 1945. There are two kinds of explanation for this. One is that the control of the state machinery of a state (any state) in the interstate system affords less real power in practice than it does in theory. The second is that there are internal class struggles going on in the states who have already known "national liberation." These two factors are linked, but it would be clearer to begin the analysis by provisionally keeping them analytically separate.

The analytical question: "How much power does one have when one has state power?" is relatively simple to explicate, once one distinguishes ideology from reality. One of the ideological principles of the modern interstate system is the totality of sovereignty. Sovereignty, or the independent juridical status of a "state" as recognized by the other state members of the interstate system, means in theory the right of the government of that state to make laws and administer its "internal" affairs without any constraints other than those that are self-imposed by the state's constitutional structure. In plain English, every government is supposed to be able to do whatever it deems wise within its borders. However, this is in fact not the case, even for such powerful states as the United States or the USSR, and *a fortiori* it is not true for the weaker states of Asia, Africa, and Latin America.

The restraints on the power of sovereign states are many.

First, there are those restraints that exist but are "illegitimate." For example, one restraint is the *de facto* power of outside forces to subvert openly or to seek to modify *sub rosa* the policies of a given state by some form of "interference" in that state's "internal" affairs. This is a familiar story. Ultimately, such an activity can involve actual military intrusion. Although in some formal sense such practices are "illegitimate" in terms of "international law," they are in fact engaged in with such frequency that any government must take cognizance of these possibilities if it intends to remain in power. Hence the threat of such illegitimate interference in practice compels a certain "prudence" on sovereign states.

Since the interstate system is normally the arena of known rivalries (for example, at the present time, that between the United States and the USSR), it is often thought that a sovereign state can "escape" the threat of interference by one strong state if it links itself politically with that state's principal rival. This is to some extent true, of course. To be sure, it then risks "interference" by the state to which it has linked itself, but it may consider this prospect less immediate and less threatening. The real question is not in this prospect. The real question lies in the realm of what might be called the "legitimate" constraints on the powers of sovereign states.

What are these "legitimate" constraints? They are those that *all* the major powers of the interstate system agree *de facto* to impose not only on the weaker states but on themselves. They are those that maintain the existence of an interstate system. These constraints are more numerous than we ordinarily recognize, primarily because they are seldom codified and are somewhat amorphous and variable in their details. They include what is sometimes called "civilized behavior" among states. For example, diplomatic immunity is a quite sacred principle, rarely violated. The social pressure to maintain this system is so strong that states often restrain themselves on matters about which they feel very strongly in order to fulfill their obligations under this principle.

A second imposed restraint has to do with trans-state property rights. The *de facto* principle is that all states may exercise eminent domain on foreign-owned property within their frontiers *up to a point.* That point is somewhat unclear. But it has not been historically true that any state could in fact nationalize without *any* compensation. Many have tried, but the counterpressures have been such that they have *all* retreated in part. A rapid look at the practices of the government of the USSR vis-à-vis foreign-property rights will make this eminently clear. (We single out the USSR only to indicate that even a state with its military might and ideology conforms to this constraint.)

A third imposed restraint has to do with the support of oppositional movements in other countries. All states (or almost all states) engage in such supportive actions. Sometimes they do it intensively. Yet they all do it only *up to a point.* There seems regularly to intrude some limit to comradely assistance. Once again the limit is unclear. But the reality is there.

If one asks how these imposed "legitimate" restraints on sovereignty really operate, often even in wartime, the answer has to be that there are implied threats of force against the violators of the norms, which are efficacious because they are supported by an exceptionally strong consensus of the world's states. Regimes that flaunt such a strong consensus rarely survive very long. When, therefore, in the early years of a "revolutionary" government, after the coming to power of a "national-liberation movement" there is a faction talking about "realism," what this faction is arguing is the need to take cognizance of these mechanisms of the interstate system. When some other movement accuses a regime that has decided to be "realistic" of being "revisionist," the accusation rings true. But the "revisionism" is structural, not volitional. Let us be very clear. We are not preaching the virtues of "realism" or "revisionism." We are merely trying to explain its repeated occurrence in states where national-liberation movements have come to power.

But this is of course not the whole story. There is also the factor of the class struggle. As long as we live in a capitalist world-economy, there is class struggle, and it continues to exist within all states located within the world-system, no matter what its political coloration. Statements of regimes that there does not exist, or there no longer exists, a class struggle within the boundaries of their state, are ideological statements devoid of analytical substance. The underlying social reality of the class struggle continues within all existing states, including those where national-liberation movements have come to power. The question is, what is the role of this national-liberation movement in relation to this class struggle in the period after it has come to power, or perhaps we should invert the question and ask what is the role of class struggle in relation to other kinds of struggle that typically characterize the capitalist world-economy, the struggle between competing "elites," that is, intra-bourgeois struggles.

There are two varieties of such intra-bourgeois struggles. One is the struggle for state power or political command. Its protagonists compete with each other (within and outside of parliaments, parties, state bureaucracies, and so on) in an attempt to seize the "commanding heights" of state apparatuses (that already exist or are being created *ex novo*) and, once in control, to enforce the sovereignty of the state. This enforcement involves struggles against other states (as emphasized in the previous pages) but also struggle against the state's own subjects.

The outcomes of the struggle among such competing political elites for state power on these three fronts (control over the state apparatus, sovereignty in the interstate system, and authority over the state's subjects) are obviously closely interrelated. In turn they are strongly influenced by the other kind of intra-elite struggle that must also be clearly distinguished from the class struggle: the struggle for the appropriation of wealth or economic command.

The protagonists of this economic struggle compete with each other (within and outside of markets and economic organizations) to obtain as large a share as possible of the wealth produced in the world-economy. The larger the share actually obtained, the larger the resources that can be mobilized in future struggles. Since "wealth" can be accumulated more easily than "state power," economic command has a cumulative character that is wanting in political command. We shall later discuss the implications of this difference. For now let us note that the difference is one of degree and that the reproduction of economic command also involves a permanent struggle on many fronts.

At the global level, the essential characteristic of the economic struggle is that each actor (normally but not necessarily a capitalist enterprise) tries to force competition upon the other actors while simultaneously creating for itself a relatively protected niche from which a rent or a quasi-rent (natural, positional, technological, organizational, and so on) can be reaped. This struggle continually structures and restructures economic activities into core activities (those that afford the appropriation of a rent or a quasi-rent) and peripheral activities (those that afford no such appropriation). Core niches are never secure for long. As soon as they are created, they invite the direct or indirect counterattack of other economic elites that have been forced by that very creation into less competitive niches. And as the counterattack unfolds, previously core activities are peripheralized and with it the locales and the organizations that hang on to them.

It follows that mobility (as among activities, locales, organizational forms, and so on) is an essential requirement for the survival/reproduction of economic elites, and this requirement often tends to bring them into conflict with political elites; despite the fact that, at the individual level, many persons move back and forth between a political role and an economic one. To be sure, the interests of political and economic elites overlap on many grounds. The very reproduction of economic elites requires the backing of political command, if for no other reason than to enforce property rights and contractual obligations; and whenever they can, economic elites are all too keen to exploit or use political command to back up or create for themselves rent and quasi-rent positions.

Conversely, political elites cannot succeed in their multi-faceted struggle for state power without the backing of the economic command wielded by economic elites. This is particularly true in view of the fact mentioned earlier that wealth or economic command accumulates more easily than political command. The implication of this difference is that success and failure in the struggle for state power is increasingly related to the actors' capability to bring (cumulating) economic command to bear upon (noncumulating) political command.

Economic and political elites are thus under considerable pressure to share/exchange the economic and political command they respectively wield. As we shall see presently, the pressure to do so originates not only in the competitive struggles for state power and wealth, but also and especially in the class struggle. When all is said and done, however, it remains true, first, that the logic of the struggle for political command is different from that of the struggle for economic command; and, second, that this difference is a source of conflict and struggle between (as well as among) political and economic elites.

For one thing, conflicts are bound to arise over the

"terms of exchange" between political and economic command. The fact that both types of elite benefit from the exchange does not in and of itself determine the terms at which the two parties will agree to carry out the exchange. A more or less wide zone of indeterminacy remains, and both types of elite will be under the pressure of their respective competitive struggles to strike the best possible bargain and, if pressed too hard, to transform the bargaining process into open conflict.

What makes this transformation likely is the fact that political command is typically "territorial" (in the sense that it is bound to a given territory) while economic command is very often, and particularly for major actors, "transterritorial" (in the sense that it operates across territories). In this case too, the difference between the two types of command is one of degree. Yet is is real enough, and it leads to a permanent struggle between political and economic elites over the "transterritoriality" of the latter, that is, their ability to move in and out of state jurisdictions rather than being permanently and completely subjected to any one of them.

All these inter- and intra-elite struggles are often confusingly discussed as though they were part of the class struggle. In our view, it is more useful to restrict the concept of class struggle to vertical conflicts that counterpose groups and individuals in situations differently related to the means of production. Inter- and intra-elite conflicts, in contrast, are typically horizontal conflicts that counterpose groups and individuals related in similar ways to the means of production or to the means of legitimate violence. As such, they are better referred to as competitive struggles and labeled as either economic or political intra-elite struggles depending on whether the primary object of the competition is wealth or state power.

Strictly speaking, in order to be able to speak of the existence of class struggle, three conditions must be fulfilled. First, there is an identifiable pattern of collective or generalized protest. Second, the objectives or the forms of the protest are such that the struggle is traceable to a class situation (that is, a given relationship to the means of production) of the participants in the protest. Third, the struggle derives from, or creates a counterposition between, groups differently related to the means of production.

According to these criteria some struggles (strikes and other forms of collective or generalized workplace protest by wage workers, the witholding of agricultural surpluses or the cutting down of cultivation by peasants or farmers, the seizure of land by landless peasants, food riots by the urban unemployed, and so on) have a strong likelihood of qualifying as episodes of class struggle. In other cases (demonstrations, urban and rural guerrilla warfare, acts of terrorism, and so on), whether or not the acts of protest qualify as episodes of the class struggle depends, among other things, on their context, protagonists, objectives, and so on. The problem in these latter instances is that the form of struggle is more frequently associated with a competitive struggle among political elites than it is with a class struggle in the sense we have defined it.

The two types of struggle can of course intersect and overlap, and they normally do. Quite often, the class struggle generates demands for leadership and organization that are supplied either by new political elites that emerge out of the class struggle itself or by previously existing elites. In either case the class struggle "flows out" into a competitive struggle for state power. As this occurs, the political elites that provide social classes with leadership and organization (even if they sincerely consider themselves "instruments" of the class struggle) usually find that they have to play by the rules of that competition and therefore must attempt to subordinate the class struggle to those rules in order to survive as competitors for state power. Conversely, it often happens that the inter- and intra-elite struggles over political and economic command wittingly or unwittingly stir up the class struggle. In this case, a particular class struggle that emerges initially as an "instrument" of intra- and inter-elite competition may very well subsequently develop its own momentum. In both instances the class struggle intersects and overlaps with the struggle over political command but remains or becomes a distinct process. *Mutatis mutandis*, the same could be said of the relationship between the class struggle and the struggle over economic command.

The Russian Revolution of 1917 was the outcome of a very special conjuncture of these three types of struggle, namely the convergence and fusion of particularly acute horizontal and vertical conflicts over world political and economic command within and across national locales. The Bolsheviks, skillfully exploiting this conjuncture, seized the commanding heights of the Russian Empire in the name of the working class. They were thereby faced with the dilemma of whether to use this newly-conquered power to sustain the class struggle within and outside their state boundaries or to consolidate their power within a restructured but tendentially stable interstate system. Although the eventual solution of the dilemma in the direction of the second vector was already foreshadowed at Kronstadt, the outcome was the result of long inter- and intra-elite struggles in which the rhetorical identification of the political interest of the Bolshevik Party and the state with the class interests of world labor played a major role in influencing and constraining the behavior of all involved.

This subordination of the class struggle in the USSR to other considerations has had two consequences. It has tended to de-legitimize the class struggle when waged against the interests of the Soviet political leadership and its more or less temporary allies. And it has promoted an ideological polarization in the interstate system that could be, and has been, exploited by national-liberation movements and the political elites that have emerged out of them. The combined effect of these two tendencies has been the continuing ambiguous relationship between the political leadership of national liberation movements and the class struggle.

In the phase of actual struggle for national liberation, that is; in the process of formation of new formally sovereign states, the political elites leading the struggles have used a double standard toward the class struggle. The legitimacy of genuine episodes of class struggle, as defined above, was upheld or denied according to whether they strengthened or weakened the elites' hand in the pursuit of the Political Kingdom. For example, whether a strike was supported/organized or not often depended on whether it was directed against the colonial authorities and sectors of capital hostile to independence, or against sectors of capital favorable to independence. This double standard was more strictly enforced when the leaderships of national-liberation movements depicted themselves as instruments or agents of the class struggle in the interstate system.

Once national independence was attained, the use of this double standard meant a further narrowing of the legitimacy of the class struggle in the new national locales. This tendency has two quite distinct roots. On the one hand, we have regimes that have attempted to consolidate their power through an alliance with the political and economic elites of core zones. In this case, the class struggle was de-legitimized as part of the political exchange between core and peripheral elites, whereby the former respect/ protect the formal sovereignty of the latter in exchange for the latter's creation within their national boundaries of an environment favorable to core capital. On the other hand, we have regimes that have attempted to consolidate their power through the opposite route of struggle against core elites. In this case, the class struggle within the country was de-legitimized as an obstacle to the former struggle, which was itself defined as class struggle at a higher level.

The fact that opposite strategies of consolidation of power led to similar outcomes from the point of view of the legitimacy of class struggle in the Third World can only be understood in the light of the peripheral position of most Third World states. This position implies little or no command over world surplus, and this, in turn, has two implications for the class struggle: (1) from the point of view of its protagonists (social classes) there is not much to be gained from it, so that actual episodes of class struggle are likely to engender frustration rather than class consciousness; (2) under these circumstances, peripheral elites competing for political command do not normally find social classes upon which to constitute reliable bases of power and hence have resorted to one of the two strategies mentioned above.

Our conception of class struggle as the pivotal process of the capitalist world-economy is thus unremarkably conventional. As struggle, it is conceived to be a struggle over the development and organization of productive forces; hence over the directional control of means of production and means of livelihood; hence over the social relations factually effecting that control. As historical process, it is conceived to be a process that continually forms and reforms the relational classes it joins in conflict. In turn, of course, their structuring, consciousness, organization, and development vary immensely, among and within the time–space structural zones of the world-scale accumulation process, owing, as was said in another context, to a "historical and moral element." As a result, the process of class struggle and the relational character of the classes formed therein continually occur historically in culturally, organizationally, and civilizationally distinctive versions, each as it were with its own authenticity and originality, which mark the scope of its historical presence. Moreover, the ongoing changes which the class struggle effects in the social structuring of the accumulation process themselves transform in locationally distinctive ways the circumstances in and through which the class struggle as historical process operates. It is as if the game and the players — there are no spectators — were always the same but the rules, officials, and boundaries of the playing field were novel on each and every occasion — and not at all that knowable until seen in retrospect.

We know from the sketch in Part I of the *Communist Manifesto* how Marx and Engels saw that class struggle formed the two great classes during the period when the ramifying social division of labor that marked industrialization of the core at that time was occurring. We know too from the European writers of the interwar period — Gramsci, Lukács, Reich, Korsch, for example — how deeply state encapsulation of the projected development of the proletariat contradicted the uniting of the workers of the world. It deflected the formative revolutionary tendencies into national and international organs, that is, into organs that work through, and so reinforce and depend upon, one of the fundamental structures and planes of operation of the capitalist economy, namely, the relational network we call its interstate system. And we know the counterpart movement: in the phrasing of E.H. Carr,

> When the cause of revolution, having proved barren in the west, flourished in the fertile soil of Asia, the shape of things to come radically changed . . . . The [Russian] revolution could now be seen not only as a revolt against bourgeois capitalism in the most backward western country, but as a revolt against western imperialism in the most advanced eastern country (1969: 30–31).

This we discussed earlier. Samir Amin drew the necessary inference for theoretical work, in remarking on the amazing power of Eurocentrism. "The vision of the 'advanced' pro letariat of the West bringing socialism as a 'gift' to the 'backward' masses of the periphery is not 'intolerable' — it is merely refuted by history" (1974: 603).

With the reestablishment of hegemony in the world-system under the aegis of the United States as hegemonic power, there developed in thought — Eastern and Western, Northern and Southern — an effort to bring class struggle and national liberation, as conceptions of transformation, into more definite *theoretical* (not merely historical) relations. We pass over here the kinds of effort we earlier called ideological in character, those where the leadership of national-liberation struggles was seen as acting in the cause of, and by some in the name of, the world proletariat's historical mission. Not many students of the capitalist world-economy today work with this sort of version, or vision, of the relation between the two constructs.

What we called the political form of the relation, however — in which the common element of struggle for state power provides the ground for considering the two, the national struggle and the class struggle, as historically alternative precursors to socialist revolution — does require brief comment. Many of us have moved theoretically in this direction if not embracing the formulation explicitly. An influential statement of the theoretical development was by Lin Biao in "The International Significance of Comrade Mao Tse-tung's Theory of People's War." There it will be recalled he first notes that "the proletarian revolutionary movement [i.e., class struggle] has for various reasons been temporarily held back in the North American and West European capitalist countries . . ." He subsequently asserts that the "national-democratic revolution is the necessary preparation for the socialist revolution, *and* the socialist revolution is the inevitable sequel to the national-democratic revolution." The national-democratic struggle has of course the form of a united front: "The revolution embraces in its ranks not only the workers, peasants, and the urban petty bourgeoisie, but also the national bourgeoisie and other patriotic and anti-imperialist democrats" (1967: 352–3 [emphasis added]).

This is not a *theoretical* understanding of the relations between national liberation and class struggle with which we can concur, as our reflections above probably suggest. There may indeed be theoretical virtue, when arraying the historical alternatives (here, futures) to which national-liberation struggles could lead (might have led, might yet lead), in the drawing of an analogy between them and the world-historical class struggle and the revolutionary transformation the conception entails. There is, however, no theoretical virtue in, and much confusion produced by, the drawing of an analogy between, (1) national-liberation struggles and the historical alternatives their attainments define and, (2) class struggle on a world scale and the historical alternatives it conceptually entails. National liberation in segments of the capitalist world-economy, and the transformations it has effected in relations of rule and other social relations, have altered the social structuring of the world-historical accumulation process. That much is historically evident and therefore theoretically to be taken into account. But it has not eliminated the relational conditions through which the accumulation process operates. And precisely that world-historical elimination, of the relational conditions through which accumulation of capital occurs, is what is entailed in the idea of the class struggle as the pivotal process in the transformation of the capitalist world-economy into a socialist world order.

Nor theoretically, in our view, could national-liberation movements, any more than core-zone social-democratic movements — given their common historical focus on securing and exercising power *within* the interstate system — have effected much more by way of change than they have done. If, however, we cease to accord strategic primacy to acquiring such state power within the interstate system, far more becomes historically possible and thereby, within the domain of historically realistic alternatives, theoretically possible. It would seem a dubious *theoretical* tenet to assert that national liberation, in its successive occurrences, is in any way a necessary condition of the revolutionary transformation of the world-economy. It is surely indefensible to claim it as a sufficient condition.

The structuring and restructuring of the world-economy in the period of US hegemony has been effected in large part by the successes of the national-liberation movements, successes that have hinged in part on the United States' becoming hegemonic, and have in turn up to a point actually furthered that hegemony, Cuba and Vietnam to the seeming contrary notwithstanding. Three aspects of that continuing change largely delimit at present both the spaces into which the class struggle as world-scale organizing process is moving, and the enclosing, fragmenting counterprocesses that have worked to prevent any "uniting" of the workers of the world.

Fundamental to the forming of the world labor-force — or in Lenin's sense, to the socialization of production, hence of the proletariat of the world — is of course the rapidly growing world-scale *technical* division of labor, through the arrangements constitutive of the operations of transnational corporations and integral, as well, to those of socially related state and interstate agencies. Fröbel, Heinrichs, and Kreye have called this "the new international division of labor" (1980). It is not to us so obviously "new," although that is as much an empirical as a conceptual matter. But it surely is not centrally "international" in the usual sense of that term. It is, rather, centrally "world-scale" — however consequential the interstate system may be in laying and maintaining the grounds for the intrafirm integrations of discrete labor processes, and the parallel structuring of accumulation, that these world-scale technical divisions of labor entail.

These continuing extensions of technical divisions of labor — of labor processes integrated authoritatively through a capitalist firm's planning and control structure, rather than through market processes — presuppose of course extraordinary centralizations of (so-called) productive capital. Theory tells us that centralizations of capital of this sort are to be expected and are likely to continue, and nothing in recent history suggests that the theory is in need of revision on this score. This growing "technical" interrelation of labor processes, through this movement of capital, interrelates as well of course the workers so associated, plus those at one remove as it were, that is, those whose productive talents are put to use in providing those directly engaged in world-scale production with means of well-being (via "the home market"). (World-scale production increasingly displaces "home-market" production of course, but we leave that aside here.) It is these ligaments of capitalist enterprise on a world scale that, joining ever larger segments of the world's workers, provide one of the ramifying relational networks through which class struggle is forming the classes it joins together.

The developmental tendencies contradicting this plane of potential proletarian union are several. Those at the level of capital proper, opposing this kind of centralization, seem relatively weak (local capital, the state bourgeoisie, and so on). Those at the level of labor, on the other hand, seem strong, notably of course state policies, sentiments of nationalism/patriotism, and the like. We return to this briefly below.

A second of the aspects (of the ongoing reorganizing of the modern world-system) is relationally very different. It has to do with the continuing centralization of (so-called) financial capital, and concerns the relational networks of increasing *governmental* indebtedness. (Whether some of these relations of indebtedness concern "capital" at all, but rather concern appropriations from realized surplus [revenue] for nonproductive operations, is an important question but not one we can address here.) These relations form the (rather intricately drawn) debtor–creditor lines of struggle in the capitalist world-economy, and so do not directly entail class-forming effects (*pace* Weber). The evolving relational network seems, however, to be moving increasingly, via the interstate system, to form highly mediated but definite connections between very large groupings of debtors and very small groupings of creditors, with the groupings being partially parallel in their formation to the classes being formed by class struggle as it is moved (by capital) out along the enterprise-organized world-scale division of labor.

The mediations matter. For the appearance is that of the creation of offical debtor and creditor "states," as condition of their existence as states. And officially classified debtor states are required, on pain of losing their creditability as states (and hence of losing, in today's world, their very "stateness"), to reduce the cost of their exports by reducing the costs to capital, direct and indirect, of labor within their borders. Popular demonstrations against such officially constructed austerity plans are reported almost daily. This world-level, organized pressure to depress the living conditions of the world's more and less proletarianized workers is hard to construe as other than a strategic escalation (by capital) of class struggle. It is, however, an escalation (a new scale) that is not all that easy to analyze. It occurs via rather original mechanisms, concerning an area of class struggle that is poorly understood theoretically, namely, the complex lines delimiting the spheres of necessary labor, relative surplus value, and levels of livelihood (or, normatively, standards of well-being). And it is a sort of pressure, particularly given the complexity of the relational mediations that divides peoples into overlapping rather than polarizing groupings. Whether, then, the groupings that in fact form, as the pressure deepens and spreads, will reinforce or weaken the elemental class-forming process is still to be determined.

One can speculate, however, that the more these popular

struggles focus in each national setting on whatever regime is in office, and so become focused on who speaks in the name of that national people as a whole, the more will such struggles weaken the workings of the world-scale class-forming process and strengthen the interstate system. The more, on the other hand, the popular movements join forces across borders (and continents) to have their respective state officials abrogate those relations of the interstate system through which the pressure is conveyed, the less likely they are to weaken, and the more likely they are to strengthen, the pivotal class-forming process of the world-economy. It seems unlikely, to assess the third historical alternative, that such popular struggles would directly become integral to, and in this way reinforce, the central area(s) of class struggle, except incidentally, here and there, owing to local conditions or local organizing acumen. World-historically, then, these local or regional struggles integral to the debtor–creditor relation of the world-economy of the sort we have been talking about may keep some relations of accumulation uncertain, but probably will not in themselves prove to be a step or stage in the eliminating of the accumulation process as central organizing force of the modern world-system.

The third aspect of the ongoing changes in the organizations and structures of the capitalist world-economy is the relational tendencies suggested by the "electronic village" notion. Neither of the kinds of centralization of capital previously remarked, let alone the relational structures of domination in virtue of which they could occur and operate, is *theoretically* conceivable without the kind of *material* conditions for the exercise of power that "electronification" provides. The relational networks being formed in addition to the one that we are talking about are truly extraordinarily complex. We who would study them are often baffled by their reach as well as by their operation; but so too are those responsible for and to them, whether in "commanding" or only "local" positions. On the other hand, these means of communication — constructed for information to move inward, commands to move outward — are in place and rapidly growing. They are integral to the expanding centralizations of productive capital and its corollary, the extending technical divisions of labor. And they are even more integral to the expanding centralizations of financial capital and its corollary, the expanding official debtor–creditor relational networks. These developmental conditions and tendencies are not in doubt.

And again, as Marx and Engels observed in Part I of the *Communist Manifesto*: "that union, to attain which the burghers of the Middle Ages, with their miserable highways, required centuries, the modern proletarians, thanks to railways, achieve in a few years" (1976: VI, 493). The metaphor of railways seems to be given more weight here than it can bear. But the general point is as clear as it is central to the way they conceive of class struggle as class forming: the means the bourgeoisie successively expand, in order to form and integrate discrete labor processes (both the technical and the social divisions of labor), thereby bring into relation, as well, the laborers whose activities are being interrelated.

Beyond the essentially administrative deployment of electronic means of communication is the capitalization of it as an historically increasing component of ordinary well-being, a process increasingly in direct conflict (not necessarily contradiction) with efforts by governments, in virtue of the workings of the interstate system, to define and filter for those territorially subject to their rule what is and is not information, entertainment, commentary, and so on. Just as one direction of electronification, as world-historical process, bears integrally on the central class-forming process by integrating the technical divisions of labor, so the other remarked on here bears integrally on popular consciousness of conditions of existence — of what is and is not tolerable, of what is and is not desirable — and hence on the abstruse matters of "necessary labor" and "relative surplus value."

As with the debtor–creditor relational structures, so (but even more so) with this second dimension of world-scale "electronification": We collectively lack as yet the theoretical ideas to gauge the directional impetus that this ongoing development will give to popular struggles and, *a fortiori*, to gauge the array of effects they may have on social movements forming through the structurally shifting loci of class struggle. Such theoretical understanding is therefore an urgent priority at this time if we wish to further the class struggle in this new period before us when the initial wave of national-liberation movements have more or less successfully completed the initial tasks they set themselves.

4

1886–1986: Beyond Haymarket?

The central fact of the historical sociology of late-nineteenth- and early-twentieth-century Europe has been the emergence of powerful social movements which implicitly or explicitly challenged the achievements of triumphant capitalism. These movements generated organizations (parties, unions, mass organizations) that survived long after the early mobilization stage; long enough to become in turn one of the targets of the new social movements of the late twentieth century. It is our contention that the earlier movements were shaped by the social structure of the nineteenth century, one that has been thoroughly transformed in the course of the twentieth century, and that the later movements are precisely the expression of this transformation. Whether and how the old organizations can survive in the new social context largely depends on their capacity to come to terms with the contradictions posed by the dissolution of their social base.

The social movements of the late nineteenth century were rooted in the intensification of the processes of capitalist centralization, and rationalization of economic activities. A large variety of social groups (servants and peasants, craftsmen and low-status professionals, small traders and shopkeepers), which had up to then coped more or less with the spread of market competition, suddenly found their established patterns of life and work threatened by widening and deepening proletarianization, and reacted to the threat through a wide variety of struggles. These struggles owed their prominence and effectiveness to the very processes they were directed against: the capitalist centralization and rationalization of economic activities.

In earlier periods, food riots and similar forms of protest resulted merely in localized disruptions of law and order which at most contributed to sudden accelerations in the "circulation of elites." The few struggles at the point of production — in industry or in agriculture — could most of the time be isolated and repressed or absorbed into the normal processes of capitalist competition. They remained, that is, the "private business" of the groups opposed in the struggle. The more production was socialized, however, the more the strife between labor and capital became a social problem: the very size and distribution of the social product were affected by them, with repercussions throughout the social and political system.

The main weakness of the European labor movement in the period under consideration lay precisely in the fact that the processes of capitalist centralization and rationalization had not gone far enough. By and large, capitalist production was still embedded in a social structure in which wage-labor played a limited role. As late as the beginning of the twentieth century, wage workers accounted for a majority of the active labor force in only a few states (definitely in the UK, probably in Germany, and possibly in France). In all states except the UK there were large numbers of "peasants" — a differentiated and stratified ensemble of low-status agricultural cultivators with some kind of access to the means of producing a subsistence.

In all states, furthermore, there were smaller but

nonetheless relatively large groups of self-employed artisans, petty bureaucrats and professionals, small traders and shopkeepers, and domestic servants. The social weight of these other groups was far greater than their numbers indicated, because a good proportion of the wage-labor force itself retained organic links with them and/or had strong cultural affinities with them. Organic links between wage workers and non-wage workers were primarily due to the practice of pooling incomes in households from different sources. Many wage-earners were not full-lifetime proletarians but members of non-proletarian households who sold their labor power on a more or less temporary basis. This practice was particularly widespread among peasant households which hired out the labor power of some of their members precisely in order to preserve their own viability as peasant households. Since these workers were generally in low-pay and low-status jobs, they had a strong incentive to retain their links with the peasant households as a form of unemployment, sickness, and old-age insurance as well as a source of self-fulfillment.

If the lower layers of the wage-labor force were populated by peasant workers and other part-lifetime proletarians who were the bearers of non-proletarian cultures, the upper layers were populated by full-lifetime proletarians some of whom nonetheless also continued to reproduce, from one generation to another, non-proletarian cultures. The two most important instances were white-collar workers and skilled blue-collar workers. The former carried out subordinate entrepreneurial functions such as keeping accounts, buying and selling, servicing the entrepreneur, and supervising the labor process. They were recruited among the lower strata of the professional groups, and, notwithstanding (or because of) their full-lifetime proletarian status, they tended to show an exaggerated attachment to the lifestyle symbols of such elites. This attachment was generally accompanied by strong sentiments of loyalty towards the capitalist employer, with whom they worked in close contact, and of whom they were living extensions.

Skilled blue-collar workers were the bearers of a quite different culture. They were craftsmen who wielded complex skills (partly manual, partly intellectual) on which production processes were highly dependent and on which the income, status, and power of the craftsmen, both in the workplace and in the household, rested. Consequently, their greatest preoccupation was the preservation of their monopolistic control over production know-how. This preoccupation identified their interests with those of self-employed craftsmen, made them suspicious of unskilled workers, and was a continuous source of antagonism towards the attempts of the capitalist employers to break the monopolistic practices of these craftsmen through de-skilling innovations.

This antagonism of craftworkers towards de-skilling innovations was probably the most important single factor sustaining and shaping the development of the European labor movement at the turn of the century. White-collar workers generally played a secondary and ambiguous role, while unskilled blue-collar workers generated great but shortlived outbursts of conflict. Generally speaking the movement was neither based on, nor did it generate *motu proprio*, the unity of wage-labor against capital. The protest of the various sectors was sparked by the same processes of capitalist development, but as the protest unfolded each segment and stratum of the wage-labor force tended to go in its own direction, often in open or latent conflict with the direction taken by other segments.

The fact that wage workers constituted either a minority or a small majority of the total labor force and that, in any event, the majority of the wage workers themselves still bore the stigmata of their non-proletarian origin, created serious dilemmas for the leadership of the movement. The first dilemma concerned the extent to which the rank-and-file of the movement could be relied upon spontaneously to produce realistic objectives and adequate forms of organization. The alternative, obviously, was that such objectives and organization be brought to the movement from the "outside," that is, by professional politicians constituted in permanent organizations. The Marxists, who argued the necessity of the latter solution, were in conflict with the anarchists and syndicalists in the early stages of the movement, even though within Marxism itself anarcho-syndicalist tendencies survived throughout the period. The main weakness of the anarcho-syndicalist position (and a key reason for its political defeat) lay in the fact that, given the social context sketched above, the spontaneous tendencies of the labor movement could only be self-defeating, as they not only heightened the internal divisions of the wage-labor force but also were powerless in the face of the economic and political mobilization of the non wage-labor force against the movement.

In a situation of this kind, the different and partly contradictory objectives of the movement could only be attained through political mediation and, ultimately, through control of state power. Political mediation and the gaining of state power in turn presupposed a centralized direction of the movement; and hence the creation of permanent organizations capable, on the one hand, of imparting such direction, and on the other, of operating professionally in the political arena.

Agreement on this point, however, posed a second dilemma concerning the time schedule and the means of gaining state power. Two alternatives presented themselves. On the one hand, the centralized direction of the movement could take a gradualist and democratic road, as advocated by the reformist wing of the Second International. The rationale of this position was that the minority status of the wage-labor force, as well as its internal divisions, were temporary problems which would in due course be taken care of by the further centralization/rationalization of economic activities immanent in capitalist accumulation. Hence the task of the leadership was to establish organic links with the movement, and fight the democratic battle for parliamentary power without any particular sense of urgency. On the other hand, the centralized direction of the movement could take a revolutionary and insurrectionary road, as advocated by the currents that were eventually to create the Third International. According to this position there was no guarantee that capitalist development would create more favorable conditions for a gradual accession to state power by working-class organizations. Quite apart from the fact that the representatives of the bourgeoisie and its allies could not be expected to yield their power peacefully, capitalism had entered a new stage of hegemonic rivalries and mercantilist struggles (the so-called stage of imperialism) which was bound to frustrate the expectations of the reformists, while however creating opportunities for the seizure of power by revolutionary vanguards.

Once in power, as happened in the interwar period to a revolutionary party in Russia and to a reformist party in Sweden, further dilemmas arose concerning what socialists could or should do with state power in a capitalist world-economy. These other dilemmas fall beyond our present concern, which is to point out that the social structure that generated the social movements, political dilemmas, and organizations of the late nineteenth and early twentieth centuries was thoroughly transformed in the course of the Second World War and the subsequent postwar phase of rapid economic expansion.

By the late 1960s, peasants had dwindled into insignificance in most of Europe. The number of shopkeepers, small traders, and artisans had also been significantly reduced. The number of professionals had increased but not sufficiently to make a great difference in the overall picture. The overall picture was now that between 60 and

90 per cent (depending on the country) of the European labor force had come to depend on wages or salaries for its subsistence. On the basis of this purely formal criterion, the European labor force had become as fully "proletarianized" as it possibly could.

However, in this case sheer numbers are deceptive. This "proletarianized" labor force in fact had a number of relatively discrete sections. The number of *salaried* professionals was large and growing, in most cases over 15 per cent of the population in the 1980s. Those in this group normally had a university education, reflecting the high percentage of the population attending the university (see Table I). The percentage of women in this category had been growing, although men still predominated. This group was well-paid of course, but lived primarily on its income.

The manufacturing sector of European countries employed 30 to 40 per cent of the population in the 1980s. This was true even in those few countries where the agricultural population was still over 10 per cent (see Table II). However, the manufacturing sector was divided with increasing clarity on ethnic lines. The better-paid, more skilled workers were largely male and native to the country, whereas the less well-paid, less skilled workers were disproportionately drawn from radical minorities, immigrants, guest workers, and so on, many of whom were not citizens (though this may turn out to be a transitional phenomenon). Of course, ethnic stratification of the workforce had no doubt a long history, but prior to 1945 the ethnic "minority" was largely drawn from within a state's boundaries (Irish in Great Britain, Bretons in France) which had different citizenship and voting consequences. The expanding clerical and service sector was in the process of increasing feminization with a concomitant loss of relative status and income level.

This sociological transformation has been going on for a long time. Its impact on the structure of social movements

Table I   *No. of university-level students per 100,000 in 1983*

Western & Northern Europe

Austria	2,058
Belgium	2,285
Denmark (1982)	2,159
Finland	2,485
France	2,253
German Federal Republic (1982)	2,289
Iceland	2,197
Ireland (1981)	1,731
Luxembourg	270
Netherlands (1982)	2,645
Norway (1982)	2,151
Sweden	2,701
Switzerland	1,515
United Kingdom (1982)	1,572

Southern Europe

Greece (1980)	1,250
Italy	1,981
Portugal (1981)	964
Spain (1982)	1,919

Other countries with over 1,500 students per 100,000

Argentina	1,962
Australia (1982)	2,237
Barbados	1,966
Canada	4,169
Ecuador (1981)	3,192
German Democratic Republic (1982)	2,420
Israel	2,746
Japan	2,033
Jordan (1982)	1,570
Korea, Republic of	2,951
Lebanon (1982)	2,715
Mongolia (1981)	2,235
New Zealand	2,612
Panama	2,212
Peru (1982)	2,001
Philippines (1981)	2,694
Qatar	1,678

USSR	1,947
USA (1982)	5,355
Uruguay	1,686
Yugoslavia	1,647

Source: UNESCO Statistical Yearbook, 1985, Table 3.10

has been profound. The labor movement and the socialist parties had originally been constructed around (male) workers in the manufacturing sector whose numbers, it had been assumed, would be ever growing. But the manufacturing sector levelled off in numbers and percentage in the 1960s and began a process of shrinkage. Faced with a sharply declining percentage of the labor force in agriculture and a levelling-off (and potential decline) in the manufacturing sectors, the tertiary sector has necessarily become ever more central. However, this sector in turn became ever more polarized into a salaried professional stratum and a lower-paid stratum working under increasingly "factory-like" conditions.

As the "internal" reserve labor force (peasantry, small artisans, wives and daughters of industrial workers) disappeared by virtue of actual incorporation into the urban, proletarianized labor force, the only "reserve" available became one "external" to the state's boundaries. Here, however, one must take into account the historical transformation of the capitalist world-economy as a whole. The development of national liberation forces in Asia, Africa, and Latin America had changed the world political *rapport de forces*, and above all the ideological atmosphere within which European social development occurred.

In the period 1945–60 it could be said that the social-democratic parties of Western Europe achieved a large number of their intermediate objectives: full organization of the industrial working class and a significant rise in their

Table II *Percentage of economically active population by occupation*

	Year	Prof.* 0/1	Manag. 2	Clerical 3	Sales 4	Service 5	Agric. 6	Manuf. 7–9	Other
Western & Northern Europe									
Austria	1984	13.0	5.2	15.6	9.2	10.8	9.1	36.9	0.2
Belgium	1970	11.1	4.6	12.8	10.2	6.7	4.5	45.2	4.9
Denmark	1983	17.0	3.1	13.9	6.0	12.6	2.1	29.4	15.9
Finland	1980	17.0	3.0	11.9	7.3	11.6	12.5	34.8	2.1
France	1982	14.1	0.3	17.1	7.8	10.7	7.6	30.9	11.5
German Federal Republic	1984	13.9	3.5	17.3	8.6	10.8	5.0	31.8	9.1
Ireland	1983	14.2	2.8	14.1	8.6	8.6	14.9	30.3	6.5
Luxembourg	1981	11.9	1.0	20.3	8.8	12.9	5.3	36.3	3.5
Netherlands	1979	17.3	2.3	17.6	9.6	10.1	5.6	30.0	7.5
Norway	1980	18.2	4.6	9.6	9.0	12.0	7.1	31.9	7.6
Switzerland	1980	15.1	2.4	20.2	8.2	11.3	6.5	34.4	1.9
Sweden	1984	27.3	2.3	11.9	8.0	13.7	5.0	28.7	3.1
United Kingdom	1971	11.1	3.7	17.9	9.0	11.7	3.0	40.0	3.6
Southern Europe									
Greece	1983	9.7	1.7	8.7	9.3	8.0	27.8	30.0	4.8
Italy	1981	11.5	16.0	9.6	11.1	11.1	9.3	20.7	10.2
Portugal	1982	5.9	0.8	10.2	8.1	9.1	23.0	37.3	5.5
Spain	1984	6.9	1.4	9.7	9.0	12.9	15.6	35.4	9.1

Other countries for comparison

		0/1	2	3	4	5	6	7-9	
Hungary	1980	14.7	0.7	12.0	4.9	7.1	10.0	50.6	—
Poland	1978	11.0	1.5	13.9	2.8	3.2	26.7	37.4	3.5
USA	1984	14.7	10.3	15.3	11.5	13.5	3.4	28.8	2.5
Venezuela	1983	10.2	4.0	11.2	12.7	13.3	14.1	32.2	2.3
El Salvador	1980	4.2	0.6	5.4	14.1	8.1	37.5	26.4	1.7
Egypt	1982	10.5	1.9	8.2	6.2	8.5	36.1	23.1	5.5
India	1980	3.0	0.1	3.7	12.6	4.6	53.7	18.4	3.9
Mali	1976	1.5	—	0.6	1.9	1.0	82.0	6.9	6.1

Source: ILO Yearbook of Labor Statistics 1985, Table 2B (except Finland from 1984; Netherlands, Hungary, El Salvador, Mali from 1983; Belgium and the United Kingdom from 1977).

*Full headings as follows: 0/1 – Professional, technical, and skilled workers; 2 – Administrative and managerial workers; 3 – Clerical and related workers; 4 – Sales workers; 5 – Service workers; 6 – Agricultural, animal husbandry and forestry, fisherman and hunters; 7–9 – Production and related workers, transport equipment, operators and laborers; Other – May include (varying with country): (a) Workers not classified by occupations; (b) Armed forces; (c) Unemployed workers; (d) Unemployed workers not previously regularly employed.

standard of living, plus accession to a place in the state political structure. But they found themselves to a significant degree locked into reflecting this traditional central core of the working class whose numbers were no longer growing. They found it far more difficult to appeal politically to the three growing segments of the wage-labor force: the salaried professionals, the "feminized" service-sector employees, and the "ethnicized" unskilled or semi-skilled labor force.

It seems therefore no accident that the three major varieties of "new" social movement have their social bases in these other groups: the peace/ecology/alternative lifestyle movements; the women's movements; the "minority" rights/"Third World within" movements. In different ways, each of these movements was expressing its discomfort not merely with the socio-economic structures that governed their lives but with the historical political strategy of the social-democratic (and Communist) parties in pursuing the need for change.

The basic complaint of the "new" social movements about the "old" social movements was that the social-democratic movements had lost their "oppositional" quality precisely as a result of their successes in achieving partial state power. It was argued that: (1) they supported both state policy and multinational policy vis-à-vis the Third World and the socialist world; and (2) they made no effort to represent the interests of the lowest-paid and most exploited strata of the work force. In short, the charge was that labor and social-democratic movements were no longer antisystemic, or at least no longer sufficiently antisystemic.

The initial response of the "old" social movement was to dismiss the charges of one segment of the "new" movements as coming from middle-class elements (that is, salaried professionals) who were using anti-industrial-worker arguments. As for the criticisms of other "new" movements (women, minorities), the "old" movements accused them of being "divisive" (the traditional nineteenth-century view of the labor movement).

The relationship of the two sets of movements — the old and the new — has gone through two phases thus far. The first phase runs from about 1960 to 1975. This phase was one of deteriorating relations between the two sets. The simmering bad relations exploded in 1968 and the tensions strongly reinforced a period of acute ideological struggle in the Third World — the Vietnam war, the Chinese Cultural Revolution, the many guerilla struggles in Latin America.

Several factors entered to bring this phase to an end. The fraction of the new social movements that became most "radicalized" — taking the various forms of Maoist parties, autonomist movements, urban terrorism — failed politically. This was partly because of repression, partly because of exhaustion and a thin social base, and partly because of changes in the ideological tone of struggles in the Third World (end of the Cultural Revolution in China, socialist wars in Indochina, end of "focoism" in Latin America).

The new *conjoncture* of the world-economy also had its impact. The growing unemployment in Europe along with the partial dismantling of the traditional heavy-industry sectors began to reopen for the labor–socialist movements many ideological questions that had been undiscussible in the period 1945–65. Thus the social democrats started to reassess their view of the new social movements just at the moment when the new social movements began to have some inner doubts about the validity of the "new left" tactics evolved in the 1960s.

The period since 1975 has been one of an uncertain minuet in old left–new left relations in Western Europe. The case of the Greens and the SPD in the Federal Republic of Germany illustrates this perfectly. Both parties are constantly in the midst of a medium-decibel internal debate about their relations with each other, able neither to move closer together nor to move further apart. Both sets of movements have however been more concerned with their relations to each other than to the other kinds of movements found in the socialist countries or the Third World.

We may resume what we have said thus: (1) the circumstances giving rise to the drive and partially successful organizational forms of the European left have been totally eroded by the very processes, those of capitalist development, they were created to supersede historically; (2) potentially serious (antisystemic) tendencies instead now come increasingly from social locales not central to the traditional organized forms of the European left. What, from our angle of vision, would seem to lie ahead?

The principal directional tendency of capital is its centralization on a world scale in two forms; financial pools, and technically divided and integrated labor processes. The first is effected through extraordinarily large-scale banking consortia managing "public" and "private" funds alike and mediated by such organs of the world's bourgeoisie as the IMF, the IBRD, and the BIS. The second is effected of course through the multiplying transnationalization of production under the aegis of the transnational corporation. This determining direction of capital on a world scale — oddly enough, not one that departs greatly from that projected in "the absolute general law of capitalist accumulation" — entails for antisystemic forces at least three broad consequential subordinate directional tendencies.

First, and in the present context perhaps foremost, is the ongoing relocation of labor-using manufacturing processes to the semiperiphery and hence the shift there of the epicenter of "classically" framed and conducted class conflict — direct, organized, large-scale capital–labor struggles. That epicenter, and so its historical trajectory, will hence increasingly be formed within the jurisdictions of the states of that zone, and their politics indeed increasingly reflect the transformation.

Second is the de-nationalization, in effect, of domestic ("national") labor forces. The world's workers, increasingly made into laborers under the aegis of capital, move as they always have in order to be in relation to capital, a movement sharply furthered in speed and extent by developments in communications and transportation. Marx and Engels saw the railroad as shortening to a century, for national proletariats, the time needed to achieve the degree of class organization it took national bourgeoisies, with their miserable roads, five centuries to attain. Ship, air, and electronics have for decades now been analogously forming the possibility of an organized world proletariat *within* "national" locales. The possibility is at once eliminated, however, so long as we think with the state-formed consciousness that there are "nationals" and there are "immigrants," and in that way reproduce the varieties of racism these historically formed categories inevitably entail. "National" and "immigrant" are categories of the capitalist world-economy's interstate system; they have no place (except as phenomenologically real conditions to be overcome) in the language of world-scale workers' movements.

And third is the "official pauperism" sketched in the general law, which, to estimate from recent trends in the US and Western Europe, has two principal overlapping social locales, the young and the aged (both men and women) and women (of all ages). These were, it will be recalled, the first "officially protected" social segments of labor, in country after country, in the decade or so that "Haymarket" signifies. "Welfare," too, has its contradictions. It seems likely that the "national"/"immigrant" categorization deepens the burdens of current capitalist development carried by the young, the old, and women, but it is only a deepening of the destruction of dignity, well-being, and hope that their pauperization *per se* entails.

The growing contradiction(s) between relations of rule and relations of production entail another trio of subordinate tendential or "directional" changes. Perhaps foremost here will be the growing contradiction of "stateness" in core-area countries, between forming and reforming the requisite frameworks of "capitalist development" of capital, on the one hand; and addressing and re-addressing the endless constituencies of "welfare" that that development continues to promote, on the other. The contradiction has been central to "stateness," of course, throughout the interstate system's historical elaboration; in our times it has been particularly evident in the peripheralized and semiperipheralized zones that are continually reproduced by the fundamental world-forming polarization entailed in the capitalist development of capital. In the state regimes of the core zone, governments have been largely spared the politics framed by the contradiction, essentially because coreness during US hegemony entailed a kind and degree of "revenue" flow that allowed "redistribution" without (all that much) pain. That has become, and will continue to become, less and less so. "Austerity" is the order of the day not only in Haiti, and in Argentina, but in France . . .

We must remark here in passing what this contradiction, in this form, implies for those of us who subscribe to the theoretical notion that relations of rule operate by virtue of a condition of consciousness known, since Weber, as their "legitimacy." Namely, it implies increasingly corrosive effects on the very "right" of the apparatuses of states to compel compliance with state-promulgated rules ("laws"). *This* sort of "legitimacy" crisis — endemic where "stateness" has been a historically imposed form of relations of rule (for example, via overrule) — seems likely to have initial occurrence in the ideologically distorted form of "nationals" versus "immigrants," with the rhetorical core being a matter of "patriotism" — the one defined domain of consciousness specifically formed to "legitimate" stateness, as every schoolchild, everywhere, knows without knowing. However, the structured incapacity of states to take care of their own, as it were, could so help shift modes of understanding and comprehension that the specifically legitimating domain of "patriotism" becomes secondary — but to what?

Second is the seemingly contradictory growth — contradictory to the capitalist development of capital — of "human rights" as an organizing concern of growing numbers of intellectuals and popular leaders, of various persuasions, throughout the world. To a large extent — framed, as the issue has been, almost solely in terms of relations of rule (its immediate locus of course, as "issue") — the comprehension of its emergence as reflecting the contradictions between relations of rule and relations of production (including relations of appropriation) has been slow to form. The rights of workers in the end underpin all others. Without the former, such "rights" as others may have are but certificates issued; annullable by the particular apparatus of "stateness" that forms the confrontational relation. As elsewhere in our conditions of existence, so here too does the capital–labor relation organize the terrain of confrontation and discourse.

A third tendential development is the growing "anti-Westernism" of the peoples of the peripheralized and semiperipheralized zone of the world-economy's operations. Primarily channelled in and through the interstate system, the impetus for the sentiment lies not in mere "anti-imperialist" (positively put, "nationalist") movements but rather in elemental challenges to the "Westernism," as encompassing civilization, that the capitalist development of the modern world as historical social system has entailed. This is a domain of inquiry fraught with difficulties, both theoretical and historical, for the once colonized and the once colonizing alike (specifically presuming good faith on the art of each, however central the historical divide perforce remains).

The tendency shows more fundamentally, if less clearly

theoretically, in the *question* of how relations of rule relate to relations of production. We reach here matters of very considerable civilizational depth, where even the distinction which we have been working with disappears. For the challenge, in process of realization, is to the "Westernism" of our ways of thinking — and, to short-circuit much — to our ways of conceiving of the "socialism" of a socialist world-system and so derivatively to our ways of identifying what is or is not "progressive."

In brief, in question is — assuming we're collectively and actively concerned with furthering the transformation of *the* capitalist world-system into *a* socialist world-system — "whose" socialism? That, it seems to us, is the query posed by the growing if still muted "anti-Westernism." It addresses directly the assumption that the coming socialist world-system is of Western manufacture, so to speak.

Perhaps the central question is this: how, and to what extent, can the well-organized arms of progressive movements in Western Europe, framed as they are by their current forms and immediate concerns, recompose themselves into agencies, not of national realization but of world-historical transformation? This recomposition would mean they became in the future as subversive of the interstate system *per se* as they have in the past been its products and proponents.

The centralization of capital *per se* can be neither factually nor strategically a legitimate concern of movements, it *as process* being for them formative merely of terrain, not of objective. The further processes it entails, however, produce the very politics of movement formation and growth. The first observation above, about the relocating of the epicenter of overt "classical" class struggle, implies merely a refocusing of Western European movements. The second and third, in contrast, entail the redefinition of trajectories. For the de-nationalization of domestic labor forces suggests a fundamental change, on the part of the left, as to what "national" means (thus leaving to the right the systemically formed residues of "primordial" sentiments). To accomplish the reconception will entail a degree and kind of substantive and rhetorical inventiveness not presently in ascendance within prominent movements. And the third, the increasing salience of the gender question, entails; (1) the elimination from the movements of yet another (and in a different sense) "primordial" sentiment, and (2) the world-scale generality of — hence organizational subordination to — what is essentially a reforming movement ("capitalism" being quite able "to develop" under conditions of legal and substantive gender equality). It is the further generalization, from the pauperization of women to the pauperization of people on a world scale, that is precisely the change in consciousness the very effectiveness of the organizations in core zones may help to bring about, *as part of* world-scale movements that bypass and so subvert interstate arrangements. The growing contradictions between relations of rule and relations of production will in all likelihood occasion a plethora of radical nationalist expressions and "movements." But world-scale movements, with emanations in various national arenas, may prove world historically even more consequential. At least, this is the major positive direction in which to move.

---------- 5 ----------

1968: The Great Rehearsal

What Was 1968 About?

There have only been two *world* revolutions. One took place in 1848. The second took place in 1968. Both were historic failures. Both transformed the world. The fact that both were unplanned and therefore in a profound sense spontaneous explains both facts — the fact that they failed, and the fact that they transformed the world. We celebrate today July 14, 1789, or at least some people do. We celebrate November 7, 1917, or at least some people do. We do not celebrate 1848 or 1968. And yet the case can be made that these dates are as significant, perhaps even more significant, than the two that attract so much attention.

1848 was a revolution for popular sovereignty — both within the nation (down with autocracy) and of the nations (self-determination, the *Völkerfrühling*). 1848 was the revolution against the counterrevolution of 1815 (the Restoration, the Concert of Europe). It was a revolution "born at least as much of hopes as of discontents" (Namier: 1944, 4). It was certainly not the French Revolution the second time around. It represented rather an attempt both to fulfill its

97

original hopes and to overcome its limitations. 1848 was, in a Hegelian sense, the sublation (*Aufhebung*) of 1789.

The same was true of 1968. It too was born of hopes at least as much as discontents. It too was a revolution against the counterrevolution represented by the US organization of its world hegemony as of 1945. It too was an attempt to fulfill the original goals of the Russian Revolution, while very much an effort to overcome the limitations of that revolution. It too therefore was a sublation, a sublation this time of 1917.

The parallel goes further. 1848 was a failure — a failure in France, a failure in the rest of Europe. So too was 1968. In both cases the bubble of popular enthusiasm and radical innovation was burst within a relatively short period. In both cases, however, the political ground-rules of the world-system were profoundly and irrevocably changed as a result of the revolution. It was 1848 which institutionalized the old left (using this term broadly). And it was 1968 that institutionalized the new social movements. Looking forward, 1848 was in this sense the great rehearsal for the Paris Commune and the Russian Revolution, for the Baku Congress and Bandoeng. 1968 was the rehearsal for what?

The lesson that oppressed groups learned from 1848 was that it would not be easy to transform the system, and that the likelihood that "spontaneous" uprisings would in fact be able to accomplish such a transformation was rather small. Two things seemed clear as a result. The states were sufficiently bureaucratized and appropriately organized to function well as machineries to put down rebellions. Occasionally, because of wars or internal political divisions among powerful strata, their repressive machinery might buckle and a "revolution" seem to be possible. But the machineries could usually be pulled together quickly enough to put down the putative or abortive revolution. Secondly, the states could easily be controlled by the powerful strata through a combination of the latter's economic strength, their political organization, and their cultural hegemony (to use Gramsci's term of a later period).

Since the states could control the masses and the powerful strata could control the states, it was clear that a serious effort of social transformation would require counter-organization — both politically and culturally. It is this perception that led to the formation for the first time of bureaucratically organized antisystemic movements with relatively clear middle-term objectives. These movements, in their two great variants of the social and the national movement, began to appear on the scene after 1848, and their numbers, geographic spread, and organizational efficiency grew steady in the century that followed.

What 1848 accomplished therefore was the historic turning of antisystemic forces towards a fundamental political strategy — that of seeking the intermediate goal of obtaining state power (one way or another) as the indispensable way-station on the road to transforming society and the world. To be sure, many argued against this strategy, but they were defeated in the debates. Over the following century, the opponents of this strategy grew weaker as the proponents of the strategy grew stronger.

1917 became such a big symbol because it was the first dramatic victory of the proponents of the state-power strategy (and in its revolutionary, as opposed to its evolutionary, variant). 1917 proved it could be done. And this time, unlike in 1848, the revolutionary government was neither suborned nor overturned. It survived. 1917 may have been the most dramatic instance but it was not of course the only instance of successes, at least partial, of this strategy. The Mexican Revolution beginning in 1910 and the Chinese Revolution of 1911 culminating in 1949 also seemed to demonstrate the worth of the strategy, for example.

By 1945, or perhaps more accurately by the 1950s, the strategy seemed to be bearing fruit around the world. All three major variants of the historic "old left" antisystemic movements — the Third International Communists, the Second International Social Democrats, and the nationalist movements (especially those outside Europe) — could point to notable successes: the armed struggle of the Communist parties in Yugoslavia and China, the massive 1945 electoral victory of the Labour Party in Great Britain, nationalist triumphs in India and Indonesia. It seemed but a matter of decades until the goals of 1848 would be realized in every corner of the globe. This widespread optimism of the antisystemic forces was nonetheless quite exaggerated, for two reasons.

One, the institutionalization of US hegemony in the world-system as of 1945 made possible a generalized counterrevolutionary thrust to slow down the pace of the growing political strength of the antisystemic movements. The US sought to "contain" the bloc of Communist states led by the USSR. And in Greece, in Western Europe, in Korea, they succeeded in such "containment." The US government sought to "defang" the Western labor and social-democratic parties by rigidifying historic differences between the Second and Third Internationals and by erecting "anti-Communism" as an ideological carapace. This attempt too was largely successful, within the US itself and elsewhere. The US sought to slow down, dilute, and/or coopt the political expressions of Third World nationalism and, with some notable exceptions like Vietnam, this effort too was largely successful.

Were the counterrevolution all that had occurred politically, however, its effect would have been momentary at most. A second thing occurred to dampen the optimism of the antisystemic forces. The movements in power performed less well than had been expected; far less well. Already in the interwar period, the Soviet experience of the 1930s — the terrors and the errors — had shaken the world's antisystemic movements. But in a sense Hitler and the long struggle of the Second World War washed away much of the dismay. However, the terrors and the errors repeated themselves after 1945 in one Communist state after another. Nor did the social-democratic governments look that good, engaged as they were in colonial repression. And, as one Third World nationalist movement after another created regimes that seemed to have their own fair share of terrors and errors, the optimism of the antisystemic forces began to be eroded.

While the US, and more generally the upper strata of the world-system, attacked the antisystemic movements exogenously as it were, the movements were simultaneously suffering ailments endogenous to them, ailments which increasingly seemed to be themselves "part of the problem."

It is in reaction to this double (exogenous and endogenous) difficulty of the traditional old left movements that the new social movements emerged, more or less in the 1960s. These new movements were concerned with the strength and survivability of the forces that dominated the world-system. But they were also concerned with what they felt was the poor performance, even the negative performance, of the world's old left movements. In the beginning of the 1960s, the concern with the power and the evil of the proponents of the status quo was still uppermost in the minds of the emergent new movements, and their concern with the inefficacies of the old left opposition was still a secondary consideration. But as the decade went on, the emphasis began to shift, as the new movements began to be more and more critical of the old movements. At first the new elements sought to be "reformist" of the tactics of the old antisystemic movements. Later, they often broke outright with them and even attacked them frontally. We cannot understand 1968 unless we see it as simultaneously a *cri de coeur* against the evils of the world-system and a fundamental questioning of the strategy of the old left opposition to the world-system.

At its height, and when it had reached the highest level of screeching, the new left accused the old left of five sins: weakness, corruption, connivance, neglect, and arrogance. The weakness was said to be the inefficacy of the old anti-systemic movements (the Social Democrats in the West, the Communists in the East, the nationalist governments in the South) in constraining the militarism, the exploitation, the imperialism, the racism, of the dominant forces in the world-system. The attitude towards the war in Vietnam became a touchstone on this issue. The corruption was said to be the fact that certain strata had, through the efforts of past antisystemic action, achieved certain material concessions and allowed their militance to be softened by this fact. The connivance was the charge of corruption taken one step further. It was said to be the willingness of certain strata worldwide actually to profit by the exploitation in the system, albeit at a lower level than that of the dominant strata. The neglect was said to be the obtuseness about, if not conscious ignoring of, the interests of the truly dispossessed, the real lower strata of the world-system (the subproletarians, the ethnic and racial minorities, and of course the women). The arrogance was said to be the contempt of the leadership of the old movements for the real problems of the lower strata, and their ideological self-assurance.

These were heady charges and they were not made all at once, or from the outset. It was an evolution from the mild questioning of the Port Huron founding statement of SDS in 1962 to the Weathermen in 1969 and after, or from the conventional views (if militantly implemented) of SNCC in the early 1960s to those of the Black Power movements of the late 1960s. It was an evolution from the Jeunesse Etudiante Communiste in France in the early 1960s who dared to be "pro-Italian," to the barricades of May 1968 in Paris (and the virtually open break with the CGT and PCF). It was an evolution from the Prague Spring which emerged in late 1967 to the founding of Solidarność in 1980.

When 1968 exploded — in Columbia University, in Paris, in Prague, in Mexico City and Tokyo, in the Italian October — it was an explosion. There was no central direction, no calculated tactical planning. The explosion was in a sense as much of a surprise to the participants as to those against whom it was directed. The most surprised were the old left movements who could not understand how they could be attacked from what seemed to them so unfair and so politically dangerous a perspective.

But the explosion was very powerful, shattering many authority relations, and shattering above all the Cold War consensus on both sides. Ideological hegemonies were challenged everywhere and the retreat, both of the powerful strata of the world-system and of the leadership of the old left antisystemic movements, was real. As we have already said, the retreat turned out to be temporary and the new movements were checked everywhere. But the changes in power relations effected by the movements were not reversed.

The Legacies of 1968

Four main changes can be distinguished. First, while the balance of military power between West and East has not changed appreciably since 1968, the capabilities of either the West or the East to police the South have become limited. The Tet Offensive of early 1968 has remained to this day a symbol of the impotence of capital-intensive warfare in curbing the intelligence and will of Third World peoples. Within five years of the offensive, the USA was forced to withdraw from Vietnam, and a new era in North–South relations began.

The most dramatic expression of this new era has been the frustration of the US government's multifarious attempts to bring the Iranian people back to "reason." It is no exaggeration to say that events in Iran since the late 1970s have had far greater influence on the internal affairs of the USA (notably on the rise and demise of Reaganism) than events in the USA have had on the internal affairs of Iran. This frustration is not the symptom of some peculiar weakness of the United States as world power, or exceptional strength of the Iranian state as an antisystemic force. Rather, it is a symptom of the increased national sovereignty enjoyed by Third World peoples in general since the withdrawal of the US from Vietnam. The close parallel between the recent experience of the USSR in Afghanistan and that of the US in Vietnam provides further evidence that the unprecedented accumulation of means of violence in the hands of the two superpowers simply reproduces the balance of terror between the two, but adds nothing to their capabilities to police the world, least of all its peripheral regions.

Secondly, the changes in power relations between status-groups such as age-groups, genders, and "ethnicities," a major consequence of the 1968 revolution, have also proved to be far more lasting than the movements which brought them to world attention. These changes are registered primarily in the hidden abodes of everyday life and as such are less easy to discern than changes in interstate power relations. Nevertheless, we can say with some confidence that even after 1973 (when most movements had subsided), the commands of dominant status-groups (such as older generations, males, "majorities") continued in general to become less likely to be obeyed by subordinate status-groups (younger generations, females, "minorities") than they ever were before 1968. This diminished power of dominant status-groups is particularly evident in core countries but may be observed to varying degrees in semiperipheral and peripheral countries as well.

Thirdly, and closely related to the above, pre-1968 power

relations between capital and labor have never been restored. In this connection, we should not be deceived by the experience of particular national segments of the capital–labor relation or by the short-term vicissitudes of the overall relation. What must be assessed is the likelihood that the commands of the functionaries of capital be obeyed by their subordinates over the entire spatial domain of the capitalist world-economy, and over a period of time long enough to allow for the interplay of commands and responses to affect the relations of production and the distribution of resources. From this point of view, the central fact of the 1970s and 1980s has been the growing frustration experienced by the functionaries of capital in their global search for safe havens of labor discipline. Many of the locales that in the early 1970s seemed to provide capitalist production with a viable alternative to the restive labor environments of the core zone have themselves turned, one after another, into loci of labor unrest — Portugal, Spain, Brazil, Iran, South Africa, and, most recently, South Korea. We may well say that since 1968 the functionaries of capital have been "on the run." And while this heightened geographical mobility has tended to dampen the unruliness of labor in the places from which the functionaries of capital have fled, it has tended to have the opposite effect in the places in which they have settled.

Finally, in the 1970s and 1980s, civil society at large has been far less responsive to the commands of the bearers (or would-be bearers) of state power than it had been before 1968. Although a general phenomenon, this diminished power of states over civil society has been most evident in the semiperiphery, where it has taken the form of a crisis of "bourgeois" and "proletarian" dictatorships alike. Since 1973, "bourgeois" dictatorships have been displaced by democratic regimes in southern Europe (Portugal, Greece, Spain), East Asia (Philippines, South Korea), and in Latin America (most notably Brazil and Argentina).

Alongside this crisis, indeed preceding and following it, has developed the crisis of the so-called dictatorships of the proletariat. Notwithstanding the many and real differences that set the Prague Spring and the Chinese Cultural Revolution apart, the two movements had one thing in common: they were assaults on the dictatorship of the officials (primarily but not exclusively on the dictatorship of the Communist Party's officials) dressed up as a dictatorship of the proletariat. In China, the assault was so violent and unrestrained as to deal a fatal blow to that dictatorship. Subsequently, party rule could be re-established (as it has been) only by accommodating demands for greater grass-roots democracy and economic decentralization. In Czechoslovakia, a nonviolent and restrained assault was put down speedily through Soviet military intervention. Yet, between 1970 and 1980 the challenge re-emerged in a more formidable fashion in Poland, eventually shaking the Soviet leadership's confidence in the possibility of patching up a crumbling hegemony indefinitely by means of repression and purely cosmetic changes in party dictatorship.

From all these points of view, 1968 is alive and well in the sense that its objective of altering the balance of power in the world social system in favor of subordinate groups has been highly successful. Yet, this success has been accompanied by an equally remarkable failure to improve the material welfare of these subordinate groups. To be sure, some material benefits did accrue to subordinate groups as a whole from the change in the balance of power. But most of these benefits have accrued to only a minority within each group, leaving the majority without any net gain, perhaps even with a net loss.

This tendency has been most evident among Third World states. The oil-producing states were able to take advantage of the new balance of power in the interstate system by charging after 1973 a much higher rent for the use of their natural resources than they were ever able to do before 1968. This advantage lasted about ten years. A few other Third World states have been able to step up their own industrialization by taking advantage of the relocation of industrial activities from core countries. How much of a gain this will constitute by the 1990s remains to be seen. But most Third World states, caught between higher prices for energy resources and stiffer competition from newly industrializing countries, have experienced even greater impoverishment and underdevelopment than they did before 1968.

Similar considerations apply to the other subordinate groups. Thus, over the last fifteen years the progressive breakdown of generational, gender, and ethnic barriers to the circulation of elites (which has benefitted quite a few members of each group) has been accompanied by youth unemployment, double exploitation of women, and the immiseration of "minorities" on an unprecedented scale. As for the change in the balance of power between labor and capital its benefits have accrued mostly to workers engaged in stepping up the automation of labor processes, or in servicing the expanded markets for elites, or in running the relocated plants in their new locations. For the rest, the gains of the late 1960s and early 1970s have been eroded, at first by the great inflation of the 1970s and then by the unemployment of the 1980s. It is probably too early to assess who is benefitting and who is losing in material terms from the crisis of dictatorships. But here too the preliminary record seems to indicate that the material benefits of greater democracy have accrued only to a small fraction of the population.

In all directions we are faced with the apparent paradox that a favorable change in the balance of power has brought little or no change in material benefit to the majority of each subordinate group. This apparent paradox has the simple explanation that the reproduction of material welfare in a capitalist world-economy is conditional upon the political and social subordination of the actual and potential laboring masses. To the extent that this subordination is lessened, the propensity of the capitalist world-economy to reproduce and expand material welfare is lessened too.

The history of the capitalist world-economy since 1973 has been the history of its adjustment to the social upheavals of the previous five years. The adjustment has been problematic, leading some to speak of a general crisis of capitalism, because of the scope, suddenness, and simultaneity of the changes in power relations ushered in by the social upheavals. When changes in power relations are limited and piecemeal, as they usually are, the capitalist world-economy can accommodate without difficulty imperceptible changes in the overall allocation of resources and distribution of rewards. But when the changes are numerous, significant, and simultaneous, as they were in the period 1968–1973, their accommodation involves long and serious disruptions in established patterns of social and economic life.

The inadequate access to means of production, of exchange, and of protection that characterizes subordinate groups makes the latter particularly vulnerable to these disruptions. We should not be surprised, therefore, if most members of the subordinate groups have experienced little or no improvement over the last fifteen years in their material welfare, notwithstanding, nay even because of, the improvement in their power position. One may wonder, however, whether this failure of a more favorable balance of power to deliver welfare might not be swinging the balance of power back in favor of dominant groups.

The cultural and political backlash of the late 1970s and of the 1980s against everything that 1968 stood for seems to suggest that this is indeed what is happening. While still paying lip-service to Third World solidarity, Third World states have been engaged in widespread feuding and intense economic competition among themselves. The younger generations, the women, the "minorities" have all switched, albeit to different degrees, from collective to individual concerns, while class solidarity and unity of political purpose among workers are in most places at an historical low. And in the epicenters of the struggle for political democracy, the desire for more and greater freedoms is often paralyzed by fears of economic disruption.

There is no denying that from all these points of view 1968 is dead and buried and cannot be revived by the thoughts and actions of the nostalgic few. Granted this, we must nonetheless distinguish carefully between the movements and ideologies of 1968 and the underlying structural transformations that preceded and outlived those movements and ideologies. These structural transformations are the outcome of secular trends of the capitalist world-economy, and as such cannot be reversed by any unfavorable conjuncture that might ensue from their open manifestation.

Thus, Adam Smith (1961: II, 213–31) long ago pointed out the negative long-term impact of an ever widening and deepening division of labor on the martial qualities of the peoples that are most directly involved in it. The greater specialization and mechanization of war activities themselves could counter this negative impact, but only up to a point. At the beginning of our century, Joseph Schumpeter made a similar point in support of his argument that capitalist development undermines the *capabilities* (as opposed to the propensities) of states to engage in imperialist wars:

> The competitive system absorbs the full energies of most of the people at all economic levels. Constant application, attention, and concentration of energy are the conditions of survival within it, primarily in the specifically economic professions, but also in other activities organized on their model . . . . In a purely capitalist world, what was once energy for war becomes simply energy for labor of every kind (1955: 69).

To this we need only to add that the spatial unevenness of capitalist development has tended to undermine the martial qualities of peoples precisely in those states where it has tended to concentrate wealth. Up to a point, core states have been able to counter the ensuing change in balance of power implicit in this tendency through an ever-increasing capital intensity of war. But at a certain point — as the experience of the US in Vietnam and of the USSR in Afghanistan have shown in exemplary fashion — further increases in the capital intensity of war bring rapidly decreasing returns, particularly when it comes to policing the periphery of the world-economy.

The same processes that undermine the power of core states over peripheral states over the *longue durée* of the capitalist world-system also undermine the power of capital over labor, of dominant over subordinate status-groups, of states over civil society. An ever widening and deepening division of labor makes capital increasingly vulnerable to workplace acts of protest and passive resistance on the part of subordinate workers, regardless of the level of class consciousness and organization expressed by those acts (see, in particular, chapter 1 above; and Arrighi & Silver, 1984). In order to reproduce, or re-establish, the command of capital over labor in the workplace, the functionaries of capital are induced to mobilize an ever-growing proportion of the labor force in wage activities but by so doing they revolutionize power relations between the genders and among age-groups and "ethnicities." Last but not least, the growing complexity of the division of labor within and across political jurisdictions makes the exercise of state power over civil society increasingly problematic.

These are the kinds of process that prepared the ground for, and eventually gave rise to, the movements of 1968. Being processes of the *longue durée*, their unfolding spans the entire lifetime of the capitalist world-economy. The explosions of 1968 and their aftermath can be interpreted as symptom of the fact that the system is approaching its historical asymptote. 1968, with its successes and failures, was thus a prelude, better, a rehearsal, of things to come.

1968: A Rehearsal of What?

If 1968 is analogous to 1848 as a failed world-scale revolution and as a world-historical great rehearsal, for what sort of world-revolution may it be the great rehearsal? Can we on analogy project today's underlying secular trends, specify what was new about yesterday's new social movements, and thereby sketch in advance likely trajectories of the confrontations and progressive social changes they suggest? As we move chronologically towards the 1990s and the 2000s, our historical social system, the capitalist world-economy, continues to be faced with difficulties in four principal arenas.

First, the interstate system is marked by a military stand-off between the US and the USSR and the evident inability of either to control matters of consequence in states of the periphery. Hegemony is giving way to its conceptual counterpoint, the condition of rivalry. The possible realignments of alliances between the five major actors — the US, the USSR, Western Europe, Japan, and China — are only now beginning. And everyone is approaching such realignments most gingerly and most fearfully. Hence, US hegemony is being eroded without any clear, and therefore reassuring, world order to replace it. Meanwhile, markets of all sorts — capital, capital goods, labor, wage-goods (ordinary), wage-goods ("durable") — are evolving at a rapid pace. They are becoming less and less regulated social mechanisms of the circuits of capital and more and more loci of speculation (what liberals call "market forces") and increasingly show (as on 19 October 1987 in equity prices) the kind of jagged price movements which are at once their hallmark and the reason for their always and everywhere being objects of regulation.

Possibly the Group of Seven (with the IBRD, IMF, and BIS) can impose renewed order. Possibly the transnationals' ingestion of markets through vertical integration (and the analogous organization of their counterparts in countries of existing socialism) is sufficient for them to absorb and so to dampen the price movements. Whether, in this sense, the world-scale centralizing of capital is historically far enough advanced (as suggested by "the absolute general law") to replace the interstate system's market-regulation via hegemony, we shall all see.

Second, the contradiction between labor and capital, given both the increasing centralization of capital and the increasing marginalization of large sectors of the labor force, will remain elemental. The new social movements have increased the worldwide pressure for higher wage-levels with world capital seeking ever more to respond to this pressure by reducing the size of labor input. As a result, there has perforce been a rising level of material well-being for a significant sector of workers and a deepening relative immiseration of many others, hence an absolute and relative increase in the inequalities of well-being among the world's workers. There has been thus a widening scope for the mechanism of unequal exchange in world-scale accumulation.

At the same time, capital's increasing search for safe havens from organized labor unrest carries with it of course a growing relocation of industrial proletarianization and hence of collective efforts to control that process and/or to ameliorate its effects. The net result may well be an increasingly class-conscious focus to the nationalist sentiment that pervades the zones outside the core, particularly in semi-peripheral states (see chapter 3 above). Similar phenomena are increasingly occurring is socialist states, notably (but certainly not only) in Poland.

Third, the ability of states to control their civil societies is diminishing. Historically, it is through the constitution of civil society, and its subsequent extension — notably, through the 1848-engendered "incorporation of the working classes into society" of the late nineteenth and early twentieth centuries — that one traces the successive transformations of the monarchies and patriciates of the nascent capitalist world-economy into its constituent and still evolving states. The organizing contradiction from the inception of stateness, state power versus civil rights and liberties, remains central to the state–civil society relation. Over time, of course, the scope of each has greatly expanded, thus sharpening the struggle, which the post-1968 world-scale "human rights" movements profoundly reflect. The notion that ruling strata seek to legitimate their rule — so that they are as morally obligated to command as those they claim to rule are morally obligated to comply — is both very old and very widespread.

Weber's central theoretical claim (1968: I, 212–307) — that certain beliefs in popular consciousness are an indispensable condition of routine compliance and so of the "stability" of the relational network administering the rules — remains plausible. However, the very increase in the efficiency of the ways in which each state controls its civil society, the expansion of an instrumental bureaucracy, itself creates the limits of its efficacy by generating an ever more widespread skepticism among those whom the bureaucracy is administering. The reach of authority has come to be more and more denied, as both the US and USSR governments among others, have increasingly discovered. 1968 symbolized the outburst of such skepticism. For a while, the coming to state power of old social movements limited this corrosion of authority. But these new regimes were quickly swept up in the increasingly "anti-state" consciousness of the mass of the population.

This process has been spectacularly abetted by the

impact of new technology on the ability of states to control their space. Electronification is physically different from electrification and does not so much abridge the space of social relations as abridge the capacity to control social relations through controlling their space. The implications for stateness remain to be explicated — and experienced. But the control of populations through controlling the space they and their relations with one another occupy — as citizenry, as communities, as individuals — is in the process of being fundamentally undermined in the two key directions formed by the modern world-system's spatial jurisdictions; within states and between states.

Fourth, the demands of the disadvantaged status-groups — of gender, of generation, of ethnicity, of race, of sexuality — will get ever stronger. We must hear Gallaudet here and add the physically handicapped, who comprise the true pariah stratum of historical capitalism. All six status-group relations are deeply different one from another, and even more so in their specificities in the world's social structures, but they share three features. Each was a ground of a new left reproach of the old left. Each in a very real sense is as much a contradiction among the people as an element of the capital–labor or state–civil society contradiction. And the oppressed of each explicitly seek not the turning of the tables but social equality, not only structurally but ideologically as well (in the sense of the elimination from social consciousness of *presumptions* of superiority/inferiority in relations of gender, generation, ethnicity, race, sexuality, able-bodiedness).

We therefore project probable realignments in the alliance systems of the interstate system along with increased sharp economic fluctuations, a sharpened (and in particular a geographically widened) class struggle, an increasing inability of states to control their civil societies, and a persistent reinforcement of the claims to equality by all the disadvantaged status-groups. It is very unclear, in the nature of things, where this will lead. After 1848, the world's old left were sure that 1917 would occur. They argued about how and where and when. But the middle-range objective of popular sovereignty was clear. After 1968, the world's antisystemic movements — the old and the new ones together — showed rather less clarity about the middle-range objective. They have tended therefore to concentrate on short-range ones. There is clearly a danger that if organizations concentrate on short-range objectives, even in the name of long-range ideals, they may sacrifice middle-range success or even middle-run survival.

We have no answer to the question: 1968, rehearsal for what? In a sense, the answers depend on the ways in which the worldwide family of antisystemic movements will rethink its middle-run strategy in the ten or twenty years to come. 1917, for good or ill, was the result of an enormous amount of collective and conscious effort by the world's old left in the years following 1848. No doubt it was also the result of structural developments in the capitalist world-economy. But it would not have happened without human organization and revolutionary programs.

The risks of drifting are very clear. The tenants of the status quo have not given up, however much their position is weakened structurally and ideologically. They still have enormous power and are using it to reconstruct a new inegalitarian world order. They could succeed. Or the world could disintegrate, from a nuclear or an ecological catastrophe. Or it could be reconstructed in the ways in which people hoped, in 1848, in 1968.

References

Amin, Samir (1974). *Accumulation on a World Scale.* New York: Monthly Review Press.

Arrighi, Giovanni, Hopkins, Terence K., & Wallerstein, Immanuel (1987). "The Liberation of Class Struggle?" *Review*, X, 3, Winter, 403–24.

Arrighi, Giovanni & Silver, Beverly J. (1984). "Labor Movements and Capital Migration: The United States and Western Europe in World-Historical Perspective," in C. Bergquist, ed., *Labor in the Capitalist World-Economy.* Beverly Hills: Sage Publications, 183–216.

Carr, E.H. (1969). *The October Revolution, Before and After.* New York: Knopf.

Fröbel, Folker, Heinrichs, Jürgen & Kreye, Otto (1980). *The New International Division of Labour.* Cambridge: Cambridge University Press.

Hopkins, Terence K. & Wallerstein, Immanuel (1981). "Structural Transformations of the World-Economy," in R. Rubinson, ed., *Dynamics of World Development.* Beverly Hills: Sage Publications, 249–59.

Lin Biao (1967). "Mao Tse-tung's Theory of People's War," in F. Schurmann & O. Schell, eds, *The China Reader: III,*

Communist China, Revolutionary Reconstruction and International Confrontation, 1949 to the Present. New York: Vintage Books, 347–59.

Marx, Karl (1959). *Capital,* Vol. I, Moscow: Foreign Languages Publishing House.

Marx, Karl & Engels, Friedrich (1967). *The Communist Manifesto.* Harmondsworth: Penguin/NLR.

Marx, Karl (1959). *Capital*, Vol. I. Moscow: Foreign Languages Publishing House.

Namier, Sir Lewis (1944). *1848: The Revolution of the Intellectuals,* The Raleigh Lecture in History, British Academy. Oxford: Oxford University Press.

Polanyi, Karl (1957). *The Great Transformation.* Boston: Beacon Press.

Schumpeter, Joseph (1955). *Imperialism and Social Classes.* New York: Meridian Books.

Smith, Adam (1961). *The Wealth of Nations.* 2 volumes. London: Methuen.

Thompson, E.P. (1964). *The Making of the English Working Class.* New York: Pantheon.

Wallerstein, Immanuel (1980). "The States in the Institutional Vortex of the Capitalist World-Economy," *International Social Science Journal,* XXXII, 4, 743–81.

Weber, Max (1946). *Essays from Max Weber,* ed. H. Gerth & C.W. Mills. Oxford & New York: Oxford University Press.

Weber, Max (1968). *Economy and Society,* ed. G. Roth & C. Wittich. New York: Bedminster Press.

Index

Index

Radical Thinkers

Theodor Adorno
In Search of Wagner
Minima Moralia
Quasi una Fantasia

Theodor Adorno et al.
Aesthetics and Politics

Giorgio Agamben
Infancy and History

Aijaz Ahmad
In Theory

Louis Althusser
For Marx
Machiavelli and Us
On Ideology
Politics and History
Philosophy and the
  Spontaneous Philosophy of
  the Scientists

Louis Althusser, Étienne
  Balibar
Reading Capital

Giovanni Arrighi et al.
Antisystemic Movements

Alain Badiou
Metapolitics

Étienne Balibar
Race, Nation, Class
Politics and the Other Scene
Spinoza and Politics

Jean Baudrillard
Fragments
Impossible Exchange
Passwords
The Perfect Crime

The System of Objects
The Transparency of Evil

Walter Benjamin
The Origin of German Tragic
  Drama

Jeremy Bentham
The Panopticon Writings

Roy Bhaskar
A Realist Theory of Science

Norberto Bobbio
Liberalism and Democracy

Judith Butler
Contingency, Hegemony,
  Universality

Simon Critchley
Ethics-Politics-Subjectivity

Guy Debord
Comments on the Society of
  the Spectacle
Panegyric

Jacques Derrida
The Politics of Friendship

Jacques Derrida et al.
Ghostly Demarcations

Peter Dews
Logics of Disintegration

Terry Eagleton
The Function of Criticism
Walter Benjamin

Hal Foster
Design and Crime

Printed in the United States
by Baker & Taylor Publisher Services